W9-CAO-978

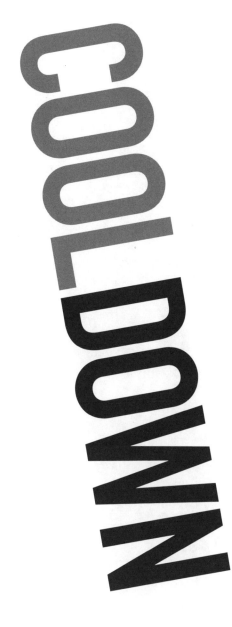

COOL DOWN

GETTING FURTHER BY GOING SLOWER

STEVE PRENTICE

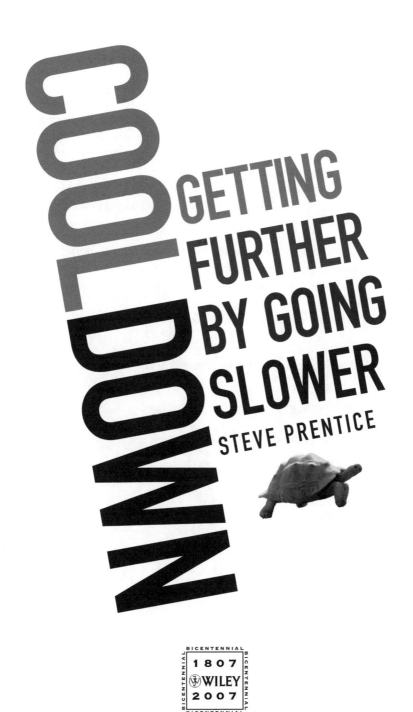

BICENTENNIAL
1807
WILEY
2007
BICENTENNIAL

John Wiley & Sons Canada, Ltd.

Copyright © 2007 by Steve Prentice

All rights reserved. No part of this work covered by the copyright herein may be reproduced or used in any form or by any means—graphic, electronic or mechanical without the prior written permission of the publisher. Any request for photocopying, recording, taping or information storage and retrieval systems of any part of this book shall be directed in writing to The Canadian Copyright Licensing Agency (Access Copyright). For an Access Copyright license, visit www.accesscopyright.ca or call toll free 1-800-893-5777.

Care has been taken to trace ownership of copyright material contained in this book. The publisher will gladly receive any information that will enable them to rectify any reference or credit line in subsequent editions.

National Library of Canada Cataloguing in Publication Data

Prentice, Steven
　　Cool down : getting further by going slower / Steve Prentice.

Includes index.
ISBN-13: 978-0-470-83902-7

　　1. Time management. I. Title.

HD69.T54P737 2006　　　　　650.1'1　　　　　C2006-905935-7

Production Credits
Cover design: Mike Chan
Interior text design: Natalia Burobina
Wiley Bicentennial Logo: Richard J. Pacifico
Printer: Printcrafters

John Wiley & Sons Canada, Ltd.
6045 Freemont Blvd.
Mississauga, Ontario
L5R 4J3

Printed in Canada

1 2 3 4 5 PC 11 10 09 08 07

ACC Library Services
Austin, Texas

To my family.

Thanks to:

Nancy Carroll, Arnold Gosewich, Dr. Jack Muskat

CONTENTS

THE SLOW MOVEMENT: WHO NEEDS IT?

Let's get this straight, right from the beginning. This is a book about the *Slow* movement, and whether it has any place in modern business. But this is not a book about how *nice* it feels to slow down and drift through life. It's a book about:

- Getting ahead
- Getting things done
- Staying employable
- Staying employed,
  and it's about
- How to do the important things fast.

Fast is important. In an age of 24/7 business, of overloaded schedules, of wireless access and a ceaseless need to stay in the loop, there isn't much tolerance among working people for a Huckleberry Finn approach to managing the day—lazy afternoons, long lunches, and taking time to observe the sun traverse the sky. We all may wish we could take this approach, but few of us have a realistic expectation of getting there any time soon. There's just too much to do, and it all needs to get done now.

Everywhere you turn you hear people talking about their ever-increasing task load; that the workday has extended to 18 hours or more; that email and wireless PDA devices are addictive and that people are using them, or are feeling pressured into using them, well into the hours that used to be reserved for personal life. This, it seems, is the new norm.

In spite of this, there are others who profess the value of going more slowly. They say they're part of a *Slow* movement. They represent a collection of organizations and individuals that together advocates working slower, speaking slower, eating slower, and basically living slower. Numerous companies, it seems, right here in North America, have actually incorporated *slow* into their infrastructure, changing work hours and office layouts to accommodate in-house daycare, workout rooms, communal meeting places, and privacy nooks. There are cities in Japan, Italy, and elsewhere that have made this *Slow* movement an official lifestyle, mandating traffic patterns, store-opening hours, and even business practices to fit with this philosophy. And, thanks to the Internet, these advocates have all joined together to become a new global-social presence.

So, is this for real? Is the *slow* approach tenable here in North America? Can it work for you, in your business, with your customers and your boss, in a way that will make things better? Sure, the Italian countryside certainly seems a good place to encourage the *Slow* movement. Workers have come and gone across its fields and streets for thousands of years. There's probably a greater readiness there to accept a shifting of gears, since, after all, Old World Europeans have "been there and done that" in so many different ways that their collective sense of time, life, and related values is by now encrusted with pragmatic acceptance. But how realistic is it to expect the *Slow* movement to catch on in those areas of the world where a high-speed work ethic reigns? It goes against instinct—against the very forces that have propelled human beings to adapt and advance. The desire to further yourself, to protect yourself and your family from harm, and to identify opportunities to improve living conditions are strong basic urges, and although, ultimately, most people work really hard so that one day they no longer have to work so much, the idea of slowing down to get there just doesn't make sense.

Julie Burchill of the *London Times* put it this way: "There is something rather sad about those people always banging on about the joys of Slow Shopping, and of its kissing cousin Slow Food; it points to dull and dreary nostalgia-hounds with too much time on their hands and a morbid fear of modernity …"[1]

So what's the answer? Does going slow appeal to you? Does it seem practical, or does it look like a recipe for "second-best"? My belief is that *slow* is not only wise, it is essential. For as the pace of life speeds up, the skills that we need to attract and build business and to maintain a superior level of productivity are getting buried under a false momentum that plays on some very deep-seated fears inside the human mind.

Furthermore, there are laws of physics that demonstrate that working faster doesn't get you there faster. But in large part, the digital age has forced us to work faster and live faster, and in so doing we have started to lose sight of the maxim "more haste, less speed."

The goal of this book, then, is to identify ways in which the concepts put forth by the *Slow* movement can be applied to ensure to your survival and success as a competitive working professional. But for this to make sense, these concepts have to be realistic. When there are 200 emails sitting in your inbox, a wireless PDA chirping on your hip, and a boss or a customer who says, "Just get it done," slowing down doesn't spring to mind as Plan A.

It's important to make the point here that not everything that is quick is bad. Responding quickly to a client's call might win new business. Solving a client's problem quickly might generate greater loyalty. Getting out of the way of a falling piano is a healthier option than just standing still. Quickness is vital to competitiveness and to survival. But quickness and quality cannot be fully achieved if everything else about your work and your mental state is hurried to the point of confusion or exhaustion. And that's why I believe this book will be valuable to you. *Cool Down* seeks to model its success strategy after people and even creatures who know the value of going slow in order to go fast. The cheetah, for example, is the fastest animal on earth. The cheetah knows so much about being *fast* primarily because she also knows about going *slow*. She knows she cannot run 70 miles an hour all day and still expect to make a catch. She knows her own strengths and weaknesses as well as those of her quarry, and is thus better empowered to strike at the right time, in the right measure.

So, ultimately, this is what I'm getting at: You can get further, faster, by incorporating *slow* into your life's strategy.

Here's how we're going to do it.

First, we'll look at some of the damage the current high-velocity, event-to-event mindset has caused, starting in Chapter 1, with an analysis of our innate fondness for, and attraction to speed. Chapter 2 observes the impact of speed on our communication and productivity within a team or work context, and Chapter 3 then looks at its costs on a personal basis. These chapters do not represent an exercise in technology-bashing. Instead they offer an opportunity to step back and observe just how human nature, technology, and globalization have combined to both bring about and then accept a massive speed-up of life, with some surprising consequences.

Next, in Chapter 4, we'll have a look at the *Slow* movement itself, to see where it came from, what its main principles are, how they compare to the ideologies of the North American work ethic, and how it has thus far been embraced by business and industry.

Then comes the big question: Should you embrace the *Slow* movement?

My answer to this is yes. I believe the adoption of *slow* principles is essential to ongoing employability for all working people. But it has to be done practically and pragmatically. First, we have to change its name, since "slow" is a difficult term for people to come to grips with. We are going to call it *cooling down*. Therefore, in all of the subsequent chapters I will demonstrate numerous ways in which *cooling down* will improve your potential and abilities, intellectually, emotionally, and creatively. In Chapter 5, for example, we look at the value of allowing your creative mind to roam more freely, unencumbered by the minutiae of the immediate, to see just what opportunities lie in that direction. My feeling is that you will be able to do more, for your future, your career and your overall happiness, by embracing the principles offered in this chapter.

Chapter 6 helps steer you towards such creative opportunities by offering advice on setting up a cooler workday—specific how-to's such as how to wake up and get up in a more productive, less stressed fashion, so that you will have time for good work, creativity, *and* exercise.

Chapter 7 offers techniques for creating a cooler, better you—how to exude charisma and confidence, how to recognize and use power in various types of situations, and how to maximize your presence in the way you talk, write, and act.

Chapter 8 looks at fear: the fear of implementing change and the fears people might have of introducing *slow* concepts into a workplace that doesn't understand them. This is important, since only by confronting fears can we work with them and through them.

Chapter 9 challenges you to apply *cool* concepts beyond the day-to-day, in order to make them part of your longer-term career strategy. This is an often-overlooked concept for busy people, for whom just getting through today can be a challenge.

Chapter 10 takes this even further by preparing you for sudden career change. Employment is not what it used to be, and sudden career change is a great likelihood for people at any level. Taking the time now to prepare for it can make all the difference between trauma and triumph.

Chapter 11 concludes the book with a look at family, which is always affected by the speed of work. Family refers not only to suburban households with kids and pets, but also to couples and singles—in essence the life outside of work that we all hope to retain and enjoy.

Cool Down is a sibling to my first book, entitled *Cool Time*, a book that explained practical time management skills from the perspective of project management, physiology, and influence rather than in terms of A, B, and C tasks. By bridging the gap that separates theory from high-pressure reality, it made time management habits real and workable for many different personality types. *Cool Down* takes this same approach to the *Slow* movement, identifying why and how the human body and mind function throughout the busy workday, and why and how a conscious approach to stepping away from reactionism, pressure, and overload is not only essential but actually achievable.

PUTTING SPEED INTO PERSPECTIVE: WHY ARE WE RACING?

A colleague of mine is the CEO of a media and design firm, and he has also been racing Porsches professionally since the age of 18. Nevertheless, he gives advice that seems contrary to the racer's image. He says, "If you want to win, you have to know how to slow down as much as how to speed up. How you enter and exit a corner will have enormous impact on your performance on the straightaway." He continues, "You have to be thinking two cars ahead. Not what the guy in front of you is doing, but the guy in front of him. The same goes for anyone driving on any highway. And you can't do that if your mind is not together and cool."

We're all driving Porsches, mentally at least, from the moment the alarm goes off in the morning until we get back into bed, 13, 16, maybe 20 hours later. But unlike professional racers, it seems a lot of us succumb to the pressure to drive in the fast lane all the time. Urged on by the persistent prodding of our wireless technologies, we feel a palpable need to extend our accessibility and responsibility well beyond reasonable limits. Many people today check their messages from their bedside the moment the clock radio announces the new morning, before their eyes have even properly focused. Many also check in as they retire to their beds at night. If they could swing it, I'm sure they would even arrange to have their email forwarded to their dreams.

A recent newspaper article highlighted the current insatiable demand for portable wireless devices, tools that, although useful, have catapulted expectation and obligation to new heights. It described a particular owner who admitted to being an addict. This person confessed to:

- Answering emails with his right hand while cleaning his teeth with his left
- Reading email one line at a time while driving
- Scrolling through his inbox while on holiday
- Scanning his email every hour or two until 9 p.m., including weekends
- Falling asleep on the sofa clutching the device to his chest. [2]

According to the article, he also admitted to using it in the bathroom and dropping it into the toilet—twice.

Twice?

Certainly, as the world becomes more and more connected, we all feel a renewed pressure to outperform, to differentiate ourselves from the competition, to do more and do it faster and usually with fewer resources than ever before. Like a giant poker game, the fear of not achieving these goals drives us forward, fueled by the constant, lurking threat that there is someone out there—a manager, a shareholder, a client, an auditor, or a competitor—who holds the final card, the ace of spades, the card of death—a person who can pull your job, your business, your identity, and your connection to the human race across the table and out of the game.

But the main point is this: No-one can hope to secure a place in either the present or the future by keeping his nose pressed tightly to the grindstone, working as hard and as fast as he can, 18 hours a day. Such behavior sits instead on the path of personal extinction.

All living species, including humans, have had to continually adapt to their changing environments. Major changes used to take thousands of years over many generations. Now substantial change happens in mere months, whether we're capable of handling it or not. I believe the next major evolutionary step for people who live and work in developed economies is to learn to manage some of the ancient instincts that have made speed so influential in their actions. We need to cool down and use *slow* as the next tool of strategic advantage. A cool mind and body provides fertile ground for creativity, providing the opportunity to deliver better solutions and circumstances, no matter what line of work we happen to be in. As newer, hungrier economies outpace us with cheaper, faster hard goods and cheaper, immediately accessible outsourced services, the act of cooling down will help us thrive, by making sure we are ready to listen actively, think clearly, work effectively, and exist proactively, keeping health and balance side-by-side with competitiveness and innovation. This is the recipe for our future. For as the pace of life continues to increase, and as jobs change and markets shift, will still be able to react—appropriately—by being mentally prepared. Quite simply, more can be done in the cool shade of clear thinking than under the hot sun of exertion and reactionism.

Consequently, we will be perceived as genuinely valuable and able to fill a need for our clients (whomever they may be) that is based as much on trust as on the quality of our deliverables.

MAKING USE OF THIS BOOK

Each chapter contains sidebars with "How To" lists, To Dos or suggestions. These are immediately useable and easy to remember. Also each chapter concludes with two valuable sections: a summary of the key issues, entitled "Key Points to Take Away," and a list of assessment questions. These assessment questions are designed to help you to observe your current habits and approaches with an eye to modifying them wherever appropriate.

If you answer each assessment question from each chapter, you will create a thorough summary of your current "self," something between a self-guided 360 and a business plan. Please note, however, that assessments and action plans are effective only when the reader undertakes three commitments:

• To write out the answers rather than just think about them
• To complete them honestly and fully
• To discuss the results with a mentor.

To help this become a reality for you, additional copies of the entire *How to Cool Down* collection with extra space for writing in your answers are available for download at the *Cool Down* section of our website: www.bristall.com. Just look for the Blue Tortoise.

1 Burchill, Julie. "Lights, action, thrills—I love my weekly romance with Tesco." *The Times Online* (2005) October 8, 2005   http://www.timesonline.co.uk/article/0,,21132-1815824,00.html
2 Calloway, Simon. "BlackBerry users press away as date nears." *The Globe and Mail* February 21, 2006.

BUSY-NESS FEELS GOOD.

DOES ALL EFFORT YIELD PROGRESS?

MIRAGES DECEIVE.

CHAPTER 1

THE ROAD TO BURNOUT

Recently a radio commercial aired for a popular brand of wireless PDA. The first voice, the owner of the device, tells how he was able to get all of Monday's work done on the train ride in. He checked his email, reviewed his PowerPoint presentation, read some documents, all kinds of great stuff. "So what happens when you get to work?" asks a second voice. "I pretend it's Tuesday," he replies, and the commercial ends.

The character in this ad is typical of many people that I have met in the business world: people who are dedicated, enthusiastic, and optimistic about their work and their career prospects. They work diligently, always alert and responsive to incoming requests for their attention and time. Their technologies allow them to compose documents, messages, and presentations much faster than just a few years ago, and the ease by which information is sent across time zones and between departments means that turnaround times are shorter, and everyone stays busy. Very busy. Yet, below the surface, these same people feel something else: a nagging sensation that speed and overload is getting the better of them. They sense a certain frustration. Their workload seems to grow all the time. There is an expectation that responses to emails and requests should be given immediately, and this occupies much of the working day. The true number of hours needed to get it all done extends into the evening and the weekend. Distraction seems to overtake focus. The stress and confusion that this causes tends to make these people feel they have to work more, just to keep up.

This is the world of speed. In principle, it makes sense. If you can do more, you advance. But the problem with speed is that is generates busy-ness as opposed to business. It brings into being a frenetic level of activity that blinds the observer as to actual progress and productivity. The constant need to "keep up" leads to a false sense of achievement, so that while we think we are swimming, we are actually just treading water.

This condition is not unique to the digital age. It has been part of organized work for many centuries, but it has truly taken a great leap forward in the last decades. It can be put into strong perspective by observing it in the light of three simple concepts, as follows:

1. PARKINSON'S LAW

Cecil Northcote Parkinson was an engineer who, in the 1950s, made a scientific study of staffing and labor in the British civil service, in which he described how the value of a department's output declined as the number of employees increased. He published his findings in a book called *Parkinson's Law: The Pursuit of Progress*. Today, Parkinson's Law is often stated as, "Work expands to fill the time available," or in terms of computers and computing, "Data expands to fill the space available for storage." In either case, the expression reflects a type of ergonomic inflation, in which scope increases, yet true productivity does not.

Were he still alive today, Cecil Parkinson would surely have enjoyed observing the way in which his law has flourished. Imagine, for example, how the rest of the day unfolds for the wireless PDA owner in the radio commercial described at the start of this chapter. He arrives at his desk having completed Monday's work on the train. His schedule, having been momentarily freed up, quickly refills with more tasks and more expectations. He now has just as much work to do as he would have if he had spent the train trip staring out the window. It's different work, but it's still just as much. So he can't really pretend it's Tuesday, because a second Monday has slipped in to fill the void. Is the new work that he takes on "high value work," or just "work"? Is he taking twice as long to work on his next project simply because time has been freed up due to his diligence on the train? Most importantly, can he tell the difference between work and productivity?

There are a great many busy people who will declare that there's nothing wrong with having two Mondays in a week. After all, that's where opportunity lies: "The early bird gets the worm," they say. But when using bird analogies, surely the size and type of worms you're after must count for something. People who remain preoccupied by incessant incoming messages and additional tasks face the danger of only ever noticing the smaller worms, while the larger ones go unnoticed, to say nothing of cats and other dangers that may also lurk nearby. When work expands to fill the time available, quality and value do not necessarily follow suit.

The neat thing about Parkinson's law, though, is that it swings both ways. Anyone who's ever had to write a term paper for school or put together a PowerPoint presentation for work knows that it usually takes right up until the drop-dead deadline to get it done, and often this means working into the late hours of the evening. But the shifting of a project's timelines can also happen in reverse. A person, for example, who decides to spring clean his house, might find it will take all weekend, *unless* he receives a surprise phone call from his mother-in-law, announcing her arrival in 45 minutes. Then, the spring cleaning will take 45 minutes. The energy allotment of a project tends to bend according to the observer's perception of the project's value.

This skewed awareness of time and work is truly quite mystical. It defines humans as unique, for although other animals are aware of time in the sense of when it's time to migrate south, when it's time to hibernate, or when it's time to sleep, these responses are governed more by internal sensations such as hunger, fatigue, and instinct. We're the only creatures that regularly troll through personal timekeeping systems, afraid equally of deadlines and empty spaces.

At the end of the day the busy person in the radio commercial will go back home on his train, and as efficient as he was in completing all of his work on the way in, the commute home will find him working on all those additional tasks that he was not able to finish during his busy workday.

2. THE PAPER CUP IN THE SLAUGHTERHOUSE

The second of our three principles comes out of the research put forth by a scientist and writer by the name of Temple Grandin. Dr. Grandin designs slaughterhouses, and she is also, by her own admission, autistic. She works with some of the nation's largest food processing companies to design abattoirs that allow animals to follow a herding instinct, rather than simply be forced to their end. Though it may seem a moot point to some, she has demonstrated and proven many economic, humane, and consumer-related health benefits to having animals avoid the stress of entrapment in unfamiliar surroundings during this difficult and final chapter of their short lives.

Dr. Grandin's autism gives her an advantage, she states, since it confers upon her the unique ability to visualize how animals process information, and by contrast, how humans do. When surveying an area in which to walk or graze, she says, an animal's attention will be inevitably drawn to any unique or unusual item or visual cue in its visual field. This item will take on a disproportionate significance in the animal's mind and will greatly impact its decision or desire to continue moving in that direction. For example, she teaches slaughterhouse employees to stay on the lookout for litter, since stray items such as a paper coffee cup lying innocuously on the floor, an item that would go unnoticed by the workers themselves, turns into a strange object of focus and fear for an already stressed cow. The cup becomes an obstacle, an irregular object, something that causes the animal to want to turn away in panic. This, she says, is also how many autistic people perceive things. They take intense interest in small singular objects, to the exclusion of all else.

The reason this is important to us in the high-speed working world is that, through the lens of her own autism, Dr. Grandin is able to tell us a lot about ourselves—the non-autistic, time-pressed working masses. She describes how non-autistic people take in information:

"Like a lamp store," she says. "Everything is on, all the time, and it's all taken in."[1] This metaphor speaks volumes about the challenge that 21st-century knowledge workers face, due to their internal wiring. For us, everything is on all the time. New stimuli, such as email, phone calls, and text messages arrive constantly and are immediately accepted as additional important elements of the day. Each of these interruptions or messages represents another lamp being lit inside the lamp store, illuminating itself inside an already brilliant cluster of lights.

We non-autistic humans are better able to handle this, we feel, because it is part of an overall multidimensional awareness machine that is controlled by the brain. Along with binocular vision, acute binaural hearing, a highly reactive sense of touch, and more deeply and mysteriously, instinct and intuition, these attributes have kept human beings alive and evolving for hundreds of thousands of years. But just as we can never see the forest when surrounded by trees, it takes the perspective of an autistic person, someone who does not share such a capacity for multiple inputs, to truly see that our predilection for a constant inflow of stimuli comes from within. It's all speed and brightness. We demand it and expect it of ourselves. But that doesn't mean we're entirely good at it.

Now, there are many who would ask, so what's wrong with speed, light, and multiple stimuli? After all, the pace, scope, and breadth of business has increased. The bright lamp store of human perception, they argue, is the hallmark of a multitasking environment, and it's up to the individual to keep up or get out. And that might be an appropriate assessment if the human body and brain were able to evolve faster, but as it is, with our body design still better attuned to finding and eating raw foods in the wild than snacks from a vending machine, there is only so much that can be pulled, both from muscles and synapses, before things give way. Every light bulb eventually burns out.

3. THE LAW OF DIMINISHING RETURNS

People who understand the rudiments of economics and business will know about the *law of diminishing returns*, the third in my list of three founding principles, and one that states that by adding more resources to a situation, there comes a time when productivity peaks and then declines. Simply continuing to add more and more resources doesn't necessarily produce consistently bigger and better returns, in just the same fashion as working more and more hours doesn't yield consistently high quality. There comes a point at which you just can't do anymore, you can't pull any more out of the day, whether you want to or not.

Yet the economists and MBAs who know all this are among those who fire up their laptops and PDAs on the train ride home, satisfying themselves that in getting one more task out of the way they can get back to the family and finally relax. They will argue that doing work on the train is an act of liberation that allows them to actually leave the office and get home in time for supper.

WHAT THESE THREE FUNDAMENTALS MEAN TO US

Parkinson's Law shows that people work on the train because they have the time to work on the train. They have allowed their working day to expand to include the hour or two so spent commuting. When people know, even subconsciously or reluctantly, that they'll be able to catch up on the train, they then allow more work to fill up the rest of the day. They may not think they're allowing it—they may feel instead that it's being forced upon them by outside powers. But that's precisely the point. Working at continual high speed with no opportunity for cooling down, they have lost a great part of themselves. They have lost the ability to set limits and negotiate around these limits. They have lost the skills needed to prioritize tasks and to say no to excessive workloads. They have lost the ability to assign realistic durations to tasks, and realistic volumes to workdays and workweeks, and they have lost the ability to educate the people they work for and to manage expectations constructively. The cushion of time that the train ride represents now becomes a solid fixture: just another hour or two in an expanded workday. When put in terms of human physiology, it's on par with noticing that your waistline is expanding and then solving the problem by buying bigger pants.

It's natural, of course, to feel justified in overworking the way we do. That's what Dr. Grandin's lamp store analogy shows us. We are wired to expect and demand multiple sources of stimulation, constantly. But as more and more of these tasks and messages insinuate themselves into the hours before 9:00 a.m. and after 6:00 p.m., there comes a point where clear, creative productive thought gets obscured for the entire day. The Law of Diminishing Returns sets in. Does an 80-hour work week truly yield 80 hours of productive work? Can anyone really be "on" for 80 hours? Is it a matter of taking 80 hours to get done what could be achieved in 60 or 40 hours were it not for the distractions of the workplace or the fatigue and overload you are experiencing? Or is it that you work for someone who expects 80 hours of dedication per week—someone with whom you have neither the time, the energy, nor the confidence to negotiate? There's nothing wrong with working hard, of course. Working hard is good. Working really hard on the wrong things is bad. When you're working so fast and furiously that you cannot spare a moment to tell the difference, that's when the problem takes root.

TIME AND STRESS

Stress, like work, is another component of the day that people accept as normal and constant: a necessary evil. It is also blamed as a major contributor to error, burnout, and illness. Indeed, one of the two major types of stress is bad for you. But another kind, as we'll see, is actually very beneficial. Can you tell the difference? Do you have the time to strategize how to avoid the bad type and encourage the good type? Have a look at this example:

Walking

There is a difference between walking fast because you like to and walking fast because you have to. If you tend to walk fast because you like it, because it matches your energy level and metabolism, or simply because you have long legs or big feet, then to walk fast is comfortable and relaxing. It's an action that you enjoy, even if it is vigorous and swift. This is an example of a positive form of stress on the body and mind, known as *eustress*. From the vigor of the action comes relaxation and a sense of cool control. From this relaxation comes a sense of freedom pacing that the brain and body truly enjoy. Thus from this positive form of *fast* (the act of walking fast) there comes a positive form of *slow*.

By contrast, when you walk fast because you have to, because you're running late and under pressure, your body and mind have to deal with negative stress, referred to clinically as *distress*, in which reaction, reflex, and haste take over, and your metabolism focuses on merely getting by. You start to sweat, to curse quietly, to wonder why you're surrounded by idiots. From this negative form of *fast* (haste) comes a negative form of *slow* (frustration, delay). No depth or progress can be achieved here, no strategy. Just coping.

When work rushes in to fill the hours available before 9:00 a.m. and after 6:00 p.m., there is a great danger of moving into this negative stress zone—working late not because we want to but because we feel we have to. Again, there are many who would respond to this by saying, "I enjoy my job, and it gives me pleasure to get some more of it done in the evening. It does not stress me at all." Or they might say, "The nature of my work demands that I be available to take a call in the evening hours. If I didn't, I would lose business to my competitors." These are fair comments. But enjoying work on an intellectual level does not guarantee a matched amount of enjoyment on the metabolic level. Similarly, though there may be complete legitimacy in taking a necessary call in the evening, the temptation then remains to continue working on the administrative elements that follow that call—elements that don't share the same level of urgency. The body needs rest. It needs an opportunity to summon up the chemicals of sleep and inject them into the bloodstream. It needs to prepare the brain for overnight shut-down, overhaul, and upgrade. We, as human beings, also need to experience activity, emotion, and interaction with significant others, children, and friends. People who continue to work outside of the working hours traditionally defined by their job may accomplish some more ground-level achievements, but they come at significant cost. The effort put in often fails to match the value of what comes out. It is a central tenet of this book, therefore, that we be able to slow down enough to distinguish between these types of actions. Can you give yourself permission to leave work behind as evening starts and allow your post-workday life to begin? Can you give yourself permission to take the important call, but then leave the follow-up parts for tomorrow? Ultimately the choice is yours, of course. But this book wishes to cut through the fog of reactionism, so that you use and maintain your most valuable commodity—yourself—optimally.

EMAIL AND MORNING VISCOSITY

Every morning, millions of hard-working men and women commute to their places of employment. For the vast majority of these people, the first thing they do upon arriving is check their email. At that moment, as the messages waiting in the inbox pour into their conscious minds they transform into reactionary beings.

There is an interesting emotional component to this morning email habit that has nothing to do with the level of importance of the messages themselves. Email is a visual medium, but it is not primarily a printed-word medium. Though the subject lines and the messages themselves consist of typed text, they appear first through a light source (the computer, phone, or PDA screen), and are therefore routed through the brain in a manner different from text on paper.

Part of the reason that email seems to have such importance to us is due to the role that the emotional side of the brain has in interpreting these visual messages. Emotional signals travel faster through the brain's internal wiring than do logical signals. You can see this in some of the expressions we use, such as "You never get a second chance to make a first impression." That's because first impressions are made by the emotional side of the brain milliseconds before a rational assessment is made. You'll get a feeling about someone or something within a fraction of a second (a concept that *Blink* author Malcom Gladwell calls "thin slicing")[2] and this judgment will frame your actions and attitudes from that point on. Even retail purchase decisions work this way. Your choice of a brand of floor cleaner will be based on an emotional assessment of the TV commercial you saw, the color of the cleaner itself, possibly recommendations from friends, and your own level of trust in the brand or manufacturer. Seldom will it be based on your knowledge of its ingredients. The same goes for shoes, cars, and restaurant reservations. These purchase decisions are rationalized only after a preliminary emotional assessment has been made. Emotion is a powerful thing.

Since incoming email messages are handled in this visual–emotional way, the body has no choice but to give them top priority. All else seems secondary, and thus this new inbound information grabs the spotlight. Many would still say "Big deal. Email is part of work, so what does it matter I handle it first?" The answer to this is best presented through another analogy: the act of pumping gas.

Pumping Gas

When do most people stop at a gas station to fill up? In the polls that we've conducted, the majority of respondents say, "When the needle starts to point towards E," in other words, when there is no other choice. A small number of respondents say, "When the price seems cheaper," which reveals they have made a conscious decision based on price. A still smaller group might have identified a pattern in gas station pricing and say, "I go to fill up late on a Sunday night or late Wednesday evening," indicating they have observed and noted a correlation between gas prices and station busy-ness.

Only a few say that they stop to fill up on their *way in* to work, since this is a very hurried time of day. Most people are already running late and cannot afford the five-minute delay unless absolutely necessary. However, they should rethink that. Gasoline is a liquid, and like all liquids, it responds to temperature variation. When gasoline sits overnight in the relative cool of subterranean tanks, it becomes a little thicker. For people who fill up their tanks in the early hours of the morning, the gas that pours through the pumps, one liter or gallon at a time, is a little more dense, which means they're getting more gasoline for the same price.[3] This is not a well-publicized feature of gasoline retailing.

This issue of early-morning viscosity applies equally well to human beings. Ninety percent of North American adults follow a circadian rhythm that orients them to morning activity. The remaining 10 percent of the population, who might refer to themselves as night owls, find their energy levels highest towards late evening. But for the majority of people, your customers and employees included, whether they feel chipper and energetic or not, the best time of the day for them is between 8:30 a.m. and 10:30 a.m., as daylight, caffeine, and the body's natural rhythms move towards the single alertness-and-energy apex of the day. This means that the *value* of the hours between 8:30 a.m. and 10:30 a.m. in terms of creativity, productivity, and mental traction, for nine out of 10 people, is far more than just the actual 120 minutes of a person's professional time. There is an intellectual viscosity here, in which more can be achieved during this period than in an equivalent two-hour time block anywhere else in the day. These hours are four-star premium time.

But what do most people do with this time? They check and respond to email. With nothing but the best of intentions, of course, they perform the ergonomic equivalent of pouring watered-down gasoline into their own gas tank. Prime creative time gets diluted by a mundane, procedural messaging system. Yes, some of the messages might be important—some of them anyway—and yes, you should respond to important ones reasonably promptly, but dealing with email *en masse* as an early morning task is like using a Ferrari to pull a camping trailer.

This is what cooling down is all about. There are better times than others to work on the important things. People need to be able to identify these times and turn them into opportunities. These are occasions in which more of the right stuff can get done at the right time. More, not less. Cooling down is not about working slower; it's about using the best of what the *Slow* movement espouses, so you can step off the carousel long enough to recognize the real strategy behind productivity.

Many people have discovered this viscosity principle on their own. They actually leave their email until after the first working hour of the day (if not the first two). They stringently defend their time against intrusion, and they negotiate rather than simply react. And you know what? They're still employed, and they're successful.

How to Make the Most of Your Morning

- Scan email subject lines, but delay responding to all but the most urgent until after 10:30.
- Use email rules to color code incoming messages to help you distinguish the truly urgent from the normal ones.
- Schedule your most important meetings for 8:30 a.m. sharp in a meeting room with plenty of natural light **OR**
- Reserve the first 90 minutes of the day to work on your most important task: Deflect other interruptions until later.
- Use this time to schedule meetings with customers.
- Use this time to schedule staff training sessions.
- Change your voicemail greeting to inform callers that you will get back to them promptly (later) this morning, and then let calls go to voice mail.

Of course, all of this depends on the requirements of a person's actual job. A frontline employee such as a help desk technician, for example, would not be wise to ignore her email first thing, if that's where the help requests come from, since in her case, these inputs constitute her primary workload. An accountant, by contrast, is a typical professional whose expertise is based on other types of tasks, and for whom email is but a communications device. What, then, would constitute the best use of his time in the morning? Obviously, it would be better spent solving his clients' problems.

But what if some of the emails in the accountant's inbox were from clients? Fear of offending the client swoops in and swiftly overrides this professional's ability to judge his own value. His need to respond speedily takes over once again, and he pushes the actual accounting work back into the less productive hours. That, once again, is the cost of speed. The speed of reaction—based on fear.

How to Set Email Aside for Later

- Use your email software's rules feature to color code incoming messages so that truly urgent ones can be seen and acted upon immediately.
- Inform your team or customers that these truly urgent messages will still be seen, and all others will be responded to promptly.
- Use your email software's rules to divert less important emails, such as general announcements, to a subfolder for reading later.

INFOMANIA AND BOXER'S DEMISE

In 1945 George Orwell published *Animal Farm*, a satire of revolution, totalitarianism, and the trappings of power, in which freshly adopted principles of equality and justice were quickly challenged and defeated as the animals of the farm grew used to their new roles. Central to the story was a horse, Boxer, who was ever willing to work harder, never giving himself a chance to rest, and most importantly, never seeing how his increased exertion was actually leading him to his own decline. He died in harness.

In the cubicles, the offices, the home offices, and mobile offices of the modern working person, a similar death in harness is happening. There's even a clinical name for it: *infomania*. Infomania describes a condition of overload that comes from attempting to handle too much information simultaneously (too many lamps in the lamp store), where the effects on the brain in terms of clear thought and problem solving skills are worse than the effects of marijuana. A study performed by psychologist Dr. Glenn Wilson at the University of London, was recently undertaken for the computing firm Hewlett Packard, and it describes what happens when people become addicted to email and text messages. The study stated that "Workers distracted by email and phone calls suffer a fall in IQ more than twice that found in marijuana smokers," adding that their researchers found 62 percent of people checked work messages at home or on holiday. "More than half of the 1,100 respondents said they always responded to email immediately or as soon as possible, with 21 percent admitting they would interrupt a meeting to do so."[4] Dr. Wilson suggested that people who constantly break away from tasks to react to email or to text messages suffer "similar effects on the mind as losing a night's sleep."[5]

Though Dr. Wilson's study may have been inflated somewhat by the media, it serves a purpose in highlighting the negative impact that distraction and busy-ness invisibly imposes on productivity. Working fast creates a type of output that requires revision, correction, and reprocessing. The lamp store of the mind, ever ready to accept more light fixtures, cannot see how its own brightness is driving customers away.

Infomania represents Boxer's death-in-harness on many human levels. It represents the death of full profitability, and the death of self-determination. It represents the loss of the chance to ever strike gold due to being mired in tedious, day-to-day work. It represents the death of enthusiasm through burnout and the death of consistent growth through high employee turnover. It represents the loss of full-life experience at home—of relationships with children, spouses, and parents, and of hobbies, passions, and leisure. It is a thankless, literally dead-end approach.

THE FLAT EARTH

The next decade and beyond will be very different for the working Western professional. The twin giants of the East, India, and China, as well as the reawakening economies of Eastern Europe, Russia, and South America are eagerly and aggressively populating the business playing field, using manufacturing muscle, high-tech skills, and ferocious enthusiasm to deliver products and services to every corner of the globe. As Thomas Freidman points out in *The World Is Flat: A Brief History of the Twenty-First Century*,[6] globalization has allowed the people of India and China to staff the call centres of the world's largest companies and speak to North American customers in well-practiced North American accents. They can do the same for Japanese customers in Japanese, right down to the local dialect. Meanwhile, to use two brief examples from Friedman's book, many U.S. hospitals routinely send X-ray and MRI images by email to India to be read and diagnosed by qualified "nighthawks" who then email their interpretations back to the requesting American physician. At the same time, accounting and law firms of all sizes are discovering that many of the services that they sell to their North American clients can be subcontracted out to these highly educated, ambitious, lower-wage professionals half a world away. Though this has actually been done by the larger firms for many years, Friedman makes the point that even corner-store accountants and lawyers—one-person operations—are now taking advantage of these same opportunities. Or at least the astute ones are. The others, those who believe their expertise to be too unique to be copied and franchised by someone in Bangalore, are instead continuing in their old ways, doing the best they can, staying responsive to the increasing speed of expectation, and all the while setting themselves up for extinction. Friedman's message is that virtually no job is safe from offshoring and globalization, and that the world is fast becoming a very different, very flat place.

Though others might argue that the threat is not as huge or as straightforward as Friedman and others contend, it remains a reality that the future for the North American professional, while not necessarily grim, will be different. Employability will be based on talents and procedures that offshore communities admit that they can't do well (yet); to be creative, for example, or to communicate closely and empathetically with clients and employees; to arrive at solutions through close attention and contact. Traditionally rigid professions such as accounting and law will have to learn to market to attract clients. Those who have seen their proprietary services opened up to wider competition will have to find out how to strengthen the bonds of loyalty in an era when loyalty is in short supply. Companies of all sizes will need to deal with higher turnover rates as employees either reject current workloads or simply fall sick and burn out. There are answers to these problems. The answers are human and intellectual. They will require, though, that we first transcend the borders of pure task orientation.

If workers spend more and more of their time in purely reactive mode, reading and responding to email, moving from meeting to meeting, keeping busy on the train as well as in the office with work that *appears* important, always behind the eight-ball of expectation, they might not notice the damage occurring and the opportunity might slip by.

Does this make sense to you? Can you perceive changes happening in your own industry? Are you interested in suggestions on how to modify your habits so you will be ready to capitalize on these changes rather than become a victim of them? If so, I invite you to read on.

KEY POINTS TO TAKE AWAY

- Parkinson's Law states, "Work invariably expands to fill the time available."
- An updated version of Parkinson's Law could be stated as "Work expands to fill the time we *think* is available."
- When people allow themselves to work beyond normal hours, more rudimentary work tends to fill the void.
- Dr. Temple Grandin is an autistic person and scientist who demonstrates how non-autistic people take in information—"like a lamp store," she says. Everything is on, all the time, and it's all taken in.
- The Law of Diminishing Returns suggests there is only so much that can be done before things give way. Every light bulb eventually burns out. There comes a time when productivity peaks and then declines. You simply can't continue to add more and more and expect consistent results.
- What is getting lost in the electronic workplace is the notion of getting value for effort. Does an 80-hour workweek truly yield 80 hours of productive work?
- Email is processed differently by the brain than are other forms of messages, which leads to a false sense of priority.
- For the majority of people the best intellectual time of the day is between 8:30 a.m. and 10:30 a.m.
- "Infomania" describes a condition of overload that comes from attempting to handle too much high-speed information simultaneously. The effects are similar to marijuana intoxication.
- The cheetah knows that being *fast* requires being strategically *slow*.
- We have to learn how to slow down enough to distinguish between productive, profitable work, and other less valuable types.
- Thomas Freidman points out that virtually no job is safe from offshoring. Employability will be based on talents and procedures such as creativity, close attention to, and contact with clients.
- People who spend more and more of their time in a purely reactive mode stand to miss out unless they slow down.
- George Orwell's horse, Boxer, symbolizes the type of "death-in-harness" that many people are facing today.

HOW TO *COOL DOWN*

The questions below are intended as a self-assessment. They work best if:

> - You actually write them out, rather than just think about them.
> - You complete them honestly.
> - You discuss the results with your mentor.

Additional copies of the entire *How to Cool Down* collection with extra space for writing in your answers are available for download at the *Cool Down* section of my website: www.bristall.com. Just look for the Blue Tortoise.

True Workload: Look Back Over Your Past Two Workweeks

- Add up all the hours you have truly given to work.
- Do you feel you often work more than the number of hours described in your job description?
- Do you take work home and work on it at home more than one day per week?
- Do you take work with you and work on it during your commute?
- How do you define multitasking?
- How productive is multitasking to you?
- How necessary is multitasking to your job?
- Do you work on the weekends more than once per month?

Identify Your Job

- What do you do?
- What does your business card describe your role as?
- How do these differ?
- How often do you review your job definition with your manager?

Deadlines: Think About a Project You Have Had to Work on Recently That Involved a Deadline

- Did you have to work right up to the deadline?
- How many times have you found yourself working right up to the deadline, e.g. 100 percent, 50 percent of the time?
- List the advantages and disadvantages that you perceive in working close to deadlines.
- On the whole, how does working to deadlines make you feel?
- What, if anything, would you like to change about this approach?
- How do you think you would do this?
- What do you think the reaction would be from managers and co-workers?

The Pace of Your Work

- What percentage of your time do you feel is taken up with satisfying the demands of the immediate?
- What percentage of these "immediate" tasks do you rate as being of top priority to your job?
- What percentage of your time do you feel is taken up with truly productive tasks?
- How does your general pace of work compare with others in your workplace? For instance, is it the norm for everyone to work at the same pace as you? Are you faster than most or slower?
- What do you do during the first hour of your morning at your workplace?
- Is this the best use of your time?
- Could you propose an alternative?

The Context of Your Work

- Can you perceive changes happening in your own industry?
- Has your company or department acknowledged or reacted to changes in your industry?

Email

- Perform an audit of current email practices, to assess when emails are responded to, and why they are responded to at that time.
- Count up the number of emails that you deal with on a typical day, including those sent, received on computer and wireless, as well as all CC copies both inbound and outbound. If you feel there is no such thing as a typical day, count up the emails that you deal with over an entire week and divide by five.
- From the totals above, calculate the cost if each email were to cost $5. (This $5 price tag better represents the cost of time lost, by factoring in the other tasks that could have been done.)

The Phone as a Business Tool

- What is your outbound voicemail policy?
- Do you change your voicemail greeting daily? Why, or why not?
- What do you think your clients feel about your current voicemail policy?
- Have you asked any of your clients (either internal or external) about your current voicemail policy?
- How do you deal with returning calls? Do you return them immediately? At set times? After work?
- What is your reasoning for your current call-return style?

Wireless PDAs and Remote Email

- Do you own a wireless, email-accessible PDA?
- How often do you check it *during* business hours?
- How often do you check it *before* business hours?
- How often do you check it *after* business hours?
- Are you able to stand still for more than a few seconds, e.g., while in an elevator, without feeling the need to check your PDA for new messages?
- Do you check your email from home after hours on a weekday?

Assessing Yourself

- When is your best time of day?
- When do you feel most energetic and charged up?
- When are you most alert?
- When are you least alert during the day?
- How many caffeinated beverages (coffee, tea, caffeinated soft drinks) do you drink in a day?
- How many times in the day have you felt "not in control"? What percentage of the day and week does this amount to?
- How could this self knowledge be applied in the scheduling of your tasks at work and at home?

Next Step: Compile this information and discuss with your mentor.

1 Grandin, Temple, PhD., *Animals in Translation: Using the Mysteries of Autism to Decode Animal Behavior*. Harvest Books; Reprint edition (January 2, 2006).
2 Gladwell, Malcom. *Blink: The Power of Thinking without Thinking*. Little, Brown and Company, 2005.
3 Proctor, Bradley, http://www.GasPriceWatch.com
4 Findings from this study were published in several media outlets, including the *London Times* and CNN. See http://www.timesonline.co.uk/article/0,,2-1580254,00.html
5 Ibid.
6 Friedman, Thomas, L. *The World Is Flat: A Brief History of the Twenty-first Century*. Farrar Straus Giroux, Expanded and Updated edition (April 30, 2006).

WE ARE CONNECTED.

BOTH WIRED AND WIRELESS WE TALK,

YET WE SAY LITTLE.

CHAPTER 2

THE SILO EFFECT

In May of 2000, the then-president of Disney, Michael Eisner, spoke to the graduating class at the University of California at Berkeley to an audience that consisted of many technically oriented new graduates. In an era when the dot-com boom was still hot, he surprised many by saying some rather unflattering things about email. He viewed it as a technology that would pose a danger to the success of companies and organizations, due to the very thing that made it popular—its immediacy. Mr. Eisner said that this would lead to a flood of unscreened emotion, with messages being sent before they were ready and information being mailed to the wrong people.

> … email is not perfect. Because it's spread so fast, it has raced ahead of our abilities to fully adapt to this new form of communication. Consider the way we learn about traditional interaction. It takes years to hone communication skills in a classroom, at a party, or when mingling in diverse company. It takes years to learn that there is a way to talk to your peers that differs from talking to your boss or your parents

or your teachers or a policeman or a judge. And now here
suddenly comes email … and, to a frightening extent, we're
unprepared.

With email, our impulse is not to file and save, but to click
and send … once we hit that send button, there's no going
back.[1]

He was right, of course, and since that speech was made, the
environment in which work is done and business transacted has grown,
with new tools, techniques, and relationships appearing regularly.
And that's where the problem lies. It has to do with the way in which
speed, combined with the act of tending to surface-level priorities,
discourages innovation. It reduces our ability to find new and better
ways to do things, to win customers, or to enhance productivity, simply
because there is so little time for reflection, communication, and shared
learning. I call this overall concept the Silo Effect, since it represents a
blinding of intellectual capacity and a reduction of the potential for full
productivity. In this chapter, I wish to illustrate the main components
that go into building our silo, so that in later chapters we can set up
some realistic plans to break the silo down and capitalize on the human
and technological brilliance of our age.

INFORMATION OVERLOAD

Information overload is not a new concept. Most people are aware of
it, have experienced it, and accept that it comes with the territory. It's
part of work. One of the primary carriers of information overload is,
of course, email. It, too, is accepted as part of work, both as a tool for
getting things done and as an obstacle to that same goal. But few know
how to deal with it properly, or why they should. It's just there, and we
use it.

The problem lies not with the connectivity aspect, but with its speed.
Email is written fast, it is sent fast, and the expectation is that we must
respond to it fast. Not only do people tend to overrule the importance
of their current tasks in order to respond to the demands of email,
the momentum that this creates carries through to other activities until

they are all processed and dealt with in a similar, hurried, surface-level fashion. Reflex and reaction start to count more than anything else.

Most people work with their email system always on, and although typical volumes of inbound messages vary from person to person, what everyone has in common is that they arrive at unpredictable times, they announce their arrival with some sort of distracting signal, and, like a tantalizing unwrapped present, they demand to be opened. Consequently, it's not a surprise that the *Infomania* study described in Chapter 1, with its headline-grabbing parallels to marijuana use, highlight a sobering fact: It's not just addiction to email that is costing us; it's the mental erosion that comes from being an information junkie that is causing the longer-term harm. People are just not able to think clearly when their brains are impaired through constant high-speed distractions.

Is email all bad? No, not at all. It's a great tool, just as a hammer is a great tool. But when it becomes a source of distraction, it descends to the same level of inefficiency as a hammer does when used by a clumsy carpenter—painfully unproductive.

There are many people, of course, who would argue strongly that email is essential to business, and that their job depends on timely response. That may be. But then again, it might not be, entirely. When people are asked to consider the nature of their email messages and what impact they have on their day-to-day success, they are often able to place the mail into two groups, with messages that are truly urgent making up the minority, and those that are not urgent making up the majority. The real answer may have more to do with a person's sense of "customer service urgency," or perhaps their fear of repercussions if the expectations of the sender are not met immediately. (The terms "customer," and "client" are used in this book to define not just external members of the business community who pay for your products and/or services, but also those on the inside—people you report to, who report to you, or with whom you interact on a regular basis.)

Great customer service *is* about getting back to the customer promptly, certainly, but it is also about getting back to him with a solution, an opportunity, something that will continue to substantiate in the customer's mind the value of doing business with you as opposed to your competitor down the street, around the world, or in the next office. Excellent customer service requires something that will further the relationship and open up new avenues of opportunity together—in a word, depth.

Information overload caused by speed also tends to obscure the notion of what *customer service* actually means. It's essential when defining this term to make sure that in addition to our own definition of the term, we clearly understand how our customers would define it. This is what Michael Eisner was referring to in his email speech quoted earlier. It takes time to learn how to communicate with, and then *know* a customer. In other words, great customer service must be based on great *customer comprehension*. Let's look at an example: Does answering an email the moment it comes in, or answering a ringing phone before the second ring constitute great customer service? It might, but then again, in some professions such reactions might be an indication that you're not busy enough, and therefore you're not the best in your field. What about people who respond to an emailed inquiry on their wireless PDA at 10:30 p.m.? Will such an action be indispensable to your customer, or will it tell him that you are working over-long hours, potentially burning out, and therefore likely unavailable for a long-term quality relationship? The point is this: Do you know where your customers sit on this issue? Have you taken the time to ask them? Or are you too busy to find out?

Speed is not the sole indicator of quality. When you go out to dinner at an upscale restaurant, you would expect the waiter to serve you immediately, because that's central to his role. But you would not expect your order to be delivered immediately. Instead, we hold to the belief that a professional, competent chef will take reasonable time to prepare and plate the meal properly, with the attention to detail that makes the dining experience at this restaurant much more enjoyable than at the fast food joint down the street. The strength of your company's reputation no doubt rests as much on the quality of your products and services as it does with the relationships you have with customers. It would be expected, therefore, that the company work to maintain this level of excellence. Information overload distorts our ability to do the research and make mindful decisions to uphold this standard. It forces people into a mental state in which they feel they *must* reciprocate at the same pace as the incoming stimulus, and that's what gets them stuck inside the silo.

Case Study: The Funeral Caller

Leanne is unhappy. Over the course of one evening, between the hours of 8:00 p.m. and 2:00 a.m., a certain client called her three times, leaving three messages and later, two emails, each with the same message. Upon returning her calls the next morning, Leanne spoke to this client, who voiced his dissatisfaction that it had taken her so long to respond. The next time the client called her, it was during the day, *during a funeral that he was attending.* Again Leanne felt guilty about not being sufficiently available.

What would you do with a person like this? How does this tie in with the ideas of customer service? What advice would you give?

Leanne's reaction was that perhaps she should be available 24/7, in order to avoid ruffling this customer's feathers again. My advice to Leanne was the opposite. I suggested she not let this trend continue. There will always be demanding people in the world, people who work at a different pace and different hours. But to fall in line unquestioningly means giving up autonomy, and worse, conditioning this person to expect the same type of treatment every time. No evening or weekend will ever be safe again. This, to me, is not customer service. It's an example of Boxer's "death-in-harness" brought about by speed. I suggested she explain to this customer that she would be happy to deal with late evening issues if they were truly emergencies, but that the high quality of work that he is paying for is best produced during the day. I would suggest also that she ask this client for more information about his timelines and priorities, in order to manage his expectations in advance rather than as they happen. By taking the time to learn more about her client, possibly identifying him as a workaholic, or merely a stressed or disorganized businessperson, Leanne would be in a far better position to anticipate his needs and prepare accordingly. This is the kind of communication and understanding you just can't get through email.

My second piece of advice was for Leanne to pause and take some time to assess this customer's overall value. Sometimes the cost of maintaining a client can be too high. Leanne was not able to grasp this until I explained that the cost should not be viewed in terms of the relationship with that particular client, but in terms of what it is doing to all of her other client relationships—the ones she can no longer maintain correctly owing to the incessant demands of this one individual. This is typical of the way in which the silo effect brought on by information overload wreaks its havoc by preventing us from seeing ourselves from the outside.

THE NEED TO STAY IN THE LOOP

The addiction to speed goes further than just the hard-wired need to respond to individual messages and clients. It has insinuated itself even further under our collective skin to the point that even when there is no email or voicemail message demanding immediate response, a craving still lurks. It's the need to stay "in the loop."

This is an obsession, a very human one. As I described earlier, a great many people yield to the temptation to check in and read their email moments before going to bed, simply because they have the technology to do so. Or they check it during their kid's school recital, or during a meeting, or in a restaurant or movie theatre. Some call in to the office for messages while driving. (This latter example, of using a cell phone while driving, has been proven to deliver the same degree of functional impairment as does a blood alcohol level of 0.08 percent, which is the standard of defining impaired driving in most states and provinces.[2]) The call of the loop even makes a walk between point A and point B feel like wasted time if our wireless PDA or cell phone is not activated and used along the way.

These people will even check into the office while they're on vacation, sometimes sending the rest of the family off to enjoy themselves, while they stay in the hotel room, tending to the loop. Surely this isn't because they find their work to be preferable to spending time with their children. It's because they fear the repercussions of not being there. Work or customer issues might escalate into problems in their absence, and then one of two things might happen:

- Either the problem gets worse because they're not there to fix it, which is going to cause further problems after the vacation is over, or
- The problem gets fixed in their absence, thereby exposing them as less-than-absolutely-essential parts of the corporate machine.

People who feel the pressure or the desire to always stay in this loop should take care to note that a loop is much like a hamster wheel, with no beginning and no end. It does not guarantee progress. Instead, it guarantees a constant revisiting of the same surface-level problems and delays, eliminating along the way any possibility for longer-term creative resolution. Such a loss of control can actually result in the obligation to stay in the loop actually being imposed by others, not just by yourself. Consider the following case study.

Mary's Interruptions and the Escalation Factor

Mary works for a large organization. Like many of her colleagues she receives a large number of emails per day from customers who have questions or requests. Many of these people send their messages with the "Read Receipt" feature attached, which informs them the moment Mary has opened and read their letter. Mary already knows that it makes sense to assign all but the most important emails to specific time blocks in the day, rather than answering each the moment it arrives. She knows all about the value and power of focus. Unfortunately, her customers don't. If they do not receive a response back within five minutes, they pick up the phone and call, and if Mary doesn't answer, they go straight to her manager. And that's Mary's fear. "If you don't stay inside the loop," she says, "the problem merely escalates to another level." Hence, the fear factor. Mary's fear of stepping out of the loop creates a silo, in which she feels obliged to respond, not just because of a hard-wired biological reflex, but because of the dangerous implications inherent in not answering. Who needs the hassle of annoyed clients, colleagues, or managers?

How to Manage the Loop

What is the solution? Well, what if Mary were to take a different tack? To use an outdoorsy metaphor, instead of spending 100 percent of her time fending off mosquitoes, would it not make more sense to buy a tent? Would it not be better if she reduced the pace of her busy week (at select times, anyway) and invested some of her time in sitting down with her manager (the one to whom the calls get escalated), to explain the reasons for her time allotments, the value of the work she prefers to focus on, her strategies for returning the customers' calls, and her plans for satisfying their needs, even if it's a few minutes or half an hour after their call? Could she not seek to get her manager on side, or perhaps collaborate towards a joint strategy? Could she not also spend a little time touching base with her mentors, either inside or outside the organization, to compare notes and to learn how others keep both their job and their sanity in the face of relentless expectations? This solution would be eminently possible, for Mary, as well as for the vacationers, and all other prisoners of the loop if they were to *cool down* and use the power of *slow* to maximize their use of human-to-human communication as a practical antidote to the speed of expectation.

Tips on Managing the Call of the Loop

- Recognize that few things are important enough to need all of your time, all the time.
- Appoint and train a "deputy" who can take and manage your calls for you in your absence.
- Leave suitable instructions at your key clients as to when you are and are not available—help them construct their days and projects around you rather than simply reacting.
- If escalation is a problem, educate your manager—get her on side.
- Always face every project by identifying the worries and concerns that your customer might have and seek to address them in advance.

- Recognize that no matter how valuable you are, the company will survive until you return.
- Remember the old phrase, "nobody ever laid on their deathbed wishing they'd spent more time at the office."
- Recognize that rest and refreshment will make you a more competent and valuable professional.

PRESENTEEISM

The ripple effect of Information Overload, combined with the fear of being out of the loop, has led to a productivity loss phenomenon known as *presenteeism*, in which people come to work even though they are fatigued, ill, or overstressed—partly out of the fear of losing their job, and partly, once again, of not being in touch with the expected momentum of their work. Presenteeism is a term coined by Manchester University psychologist Cary Cooper. He describes it as like absenteeism in all respects except for the fact that the employee in question is physically at the workplace instead of home in bed.

Employees do not have to be actually ill or paralyzed with stress to experience presenteeism. Consider:

- Secretly tending to email on your wireless PDA while in a meeting
- Attempting to focus on having a conversation with someone while your cellphone rings in your briefcase
- Trying to maintain a telephone conversation with someone, while continuing to type on your computer keyboard
- Trying to focus on a meeting or project after having worked late the night before, or while suffering from jetlag
- Trying to complete one project with the pressure of another looming clearly in your mind
- Trying to work on office-related tasks at home, while the kids are watching TV right next to you

These are all examples of presenteeism that combine our fear of repercussions with a perceived obligation to keep going inside the loop. This has led to legions of professionals showing up at their place of work every day, and despite their best efforts, they just can't function fully. The short-term results are sometimes obvious, for example, when meetings go off track or tasks are not completed on time, but sometimes they are less so, since it's not always easy to perceive optimum and sub-optimum performance when standing in the midst of it.

The Tachometer on Your Forehead

In Chapter 1, I used the example of early morning gasoline in reference to the viscosity of the thinking process at select times of the day. It is appropriate to extend the automotive analogy at this point by drawing attention to the gauge that most cars have on their instrument panel, called a *tachometer*, which indicates the number of revolutions per minute the engine is doing. There is an optimum zone at which your car has been designed to operate best, usually when it's in top gear and cruising along an open road without needing to stop and start constantly.

If we, as human beings, were able to incorporate a similar gauge on our own foreheads, one that registered the amount of our mental potential and throughput, we would hope that it stayed most of the time in a similar type of "optimum zone," perhaps within 75 to 90 percent capacity. We could really do with a gauge like that because we lack any other reliable form of quantifying mental capacity on a minute-by-minute basis. We would be surprised to learn, however, just how often the needle dips down into regions much lower than that. Distraction and disruptions force the brain's own thinking patterns to regularly re-set and rebuild. Presenteeism, caused by speed, fatigue, stress, and worry, forces the needle backwards to a zone far below what is desired and expected. Such a gauge would clearly illustrate the cost of our reaction to high-speed expectation. It's the human equivalent of driving with the handbrake on.

Can you identify presenteeism in yourself? In your colleagues? If a colleague was suffering with a fever and was obviously fading fast, common sense would tell you to send that person home. Presenteeism is not so obvious, however. It needs to be identified and dealt with, in yourself and others. This is a practiced skill.

Tips for Identifying Presenteeism in Others

- Review timesheets or other evidence of people staying overly long at their workplace.
- Observe the timestamps on emails and other messages—when are they being sent? What time of day or night?
- Observe whether your staff/colleagues are taking breaks for lunch and even to stretch and move (if their job is sedentary).
- Consult the company medical department and ask, within the bounds of confidentiality, whether there has been an overall rise in headache, stress-related, or even breathing-related complaints.
- Review the frequency of contact between workers and their managers.
- Take note of the quality of participation in meetings and conversations as well as the quality of spelling and completeness in emails.
- Take note of the same symptoms in yourself.

INTELLECTUAL ISOLATION

The fourth silo effect at work is that of intellectual isolation. This problem is best illustrated by another book, *A Whole New Mind*, by Daniel Pink, which, when paired with *The World Is Flat* by Thomas Friedman, helps paint a clear picture of the cost of improperly adapting to the changing demands of business. Specifically, Pink outlines the need for a new mindset. He demonstrates how the "other" side of the brain, the creative side, is more necessary than ever, even amidst traditionally logical detail-oriented professions such as accounting and law. He writes:

> It is an age animated by a different form of thinking and a new approach to life—one that prizes aptitudes that I call "high concept" and "high touch." High concept involves the capacity to detect patterns and opportunities, to create

artistic and emotional beauty, to craft a satisfying narrative, and to combine seemingly unrelated ideas into something new. High touch involves the ability to empathize with others, to understand the subtleties of human interaction, to find joy in one's self and to elicit it in others, and to stretch beyond the quotidian in pursuit of purpose and meaning.[3]

Pink and Freidman point to the rapidly emerging technologies that make up the wired and wireless world. These are flattening the world out, they say, allowing business to be done anywhere and anytime. And that's great, for some things. It's faster and cheaper to send digital blueprints by email than to courier the originals, but what of the synergies that would come up with a building's conception and financing in the first place? What of the human elements that go into anticipating and understanding the intangibles that always occur in every project?

Case Study: Mass Transit Chaos

Recently the mass transit rail system of a major North American city noticed something disturbing: More and more of their engineers were calling in sick on Fridays than on any other day. And when the engineers don't come to work, the trains don't roll. Though a few of these engineers could have been legitimately excused as ill, many of them had excused themselves simply because they were too tired and stressed, and believed that they could not operate their trains safely. As a result certain scheduled runs had to be cancelled, and thousands of commuters had to find alternate ways to travel. The economy of an entire city was affected.

Now on the surface this case study appears to only be about absenteeism. But it's important to observe why and how such absenteeism was allowed to develop and flourish in the first place. What if it was discovered that all of the scheduling of these engineers had been done through email or electronic calendaring? Such tools are convenient, yes, but they are also sterile. They are made up of digitized text and numbers. This creates a situation in which the managers who allocate the routes or the shifts, managers who themselves are likely overburdened, are forced to assign tasks to people they cannot see. This is not communicating. Human communication is an organic, interactive thing. It requires more than just words. As sentient creatures, we human beings take in most of our knowledge through a combination of senses. In terms of human communication this means body language (non-verbal communication), eye contact, inflection, and vocal tone, in addition to the words spoken.

A manager who is allowed the time to visit with her staff, or even talk to them by telephone might be able to pick up on subtle pauses, tonalities, or other cues that twig her to the fact that even though her employee says "yes" to a job request, the non-verbal element of the conversation tells a different story. This is an example of the "high touch" ideal that Daniel Pink refers to. It takes more time to execute, but saves more in the long run.

Case Study: How a Busy Lawyer Escapes Intellectual Isolation

Amy Schuilman, a partner in the law firm of DLA Piper Rudnick Gray Cary, is one of a dozen high-profile executives who were interviewed by *Fortune* magazine for a feature entitled "How I Work," which sought to identify just how these successful people get through their day. Ms. Schuilman revealed a terrific insight into the nature of email, cell phones, and true human connection. Even though she herself answers hundreds of emails a day, she has a system *and* a pair of assistants to help control this influx and keep it manageable. She says:

> I don't leave my cell phone on. I'm often in meetings or with clients, and I don't want people to assume that they can dial my cell phone and get me, unless it's an emergency. You can't leave it on if you're in a meeting with the CEO or a witness. It's really important to focus on the problem at hand. You get into a rhythm of a conversation, and you have to honor that

rhythm. People get anxious when they feel they're going to be interrupted. What a good lawyer brings to a problem, in addition to creative solutions, is a quality of attentiveness. You can't listen with half an ear."[4]

You see that? Rhythm! Not just book smarts, but rhythm! A knowledge of how people act and respond on a level separate from that of just words. Ms. Schuilman takes advantage of the principle of rhythm, not merely to express her own ideas, but to ensure that the person with whom she's talking does not feel stress through anticipation of being cut off. That's true human insight.

Of course, it is much easier, physically, emotionally, and time-wise, to electronically dispatch a request, a problem, an issue or an assignment to another human being, but there is no room in such a unidirectional messaging system for true discussion. And this is what I'm really getting at here. The pressure we feel to deal with issues quickly and to avoid having to take time to explain them or give them further depth makes us want to turn to fast communications first. But those very technologies actually tend to prolong the exercise or even deny its successful completion.

Case Study: Email Badminton

Bruno and Karen work for a financial services company. They both have full schedules and tight deadlines to meet. Around 3:00 p.m., Karen emails Bruno and asks him for his thoughts on a project scheduled for the spring. Bruno looks up from his work when the email arrives. The subject line says only, "Spring Promotion ideas," but since it's from Karen, his boss, he feels obliged to look at it right away. He breaks completely away from his current train of thought and opens the email. It asks Bruno for his thoughts, so he dutifully starts to pound away at his keyboard. Some of the ideas, he knows, may go against Karen's own plans, but others might hit the mark, and at any rate he feels safer putting them all in the message. "At least then, it will be on record that I suggested these things," he thinks to himself, "even if Karen shoots them down."

The email takes about half an hour to write, proof, correct, and then send, amidst other distractions that add to an already backlogged day. Finally, Bruno sends the email. Since Karen is currently stuck in back-to-back meetings and will be for the duration of the afternoon, Bruno's response sits in her inbox for two hours until she returns to her desk at 5:40 p.m. Too tired to read it now, she opts to save it for the train ride home, when she can read it at leisure from the inbox of her wireless PDA.

The train, as usual, is packed, and far from quiet. Karen starts to read Bruno's letter, but cannot think clearly. Fatigue from a long day and too many loud conversations around her make it hard to stay focused. She opts to respond to it later, after the kids are in bed. Finally, late in the evening, Karen gets around to responding to Bruno's thoughts. She keys in some thoughts and ideas of her own, some in agreement with Bruno, some with politely phrased reservation. The email is dispatched to Bruno at 11:15 p.m., and Karen goes to bed. Still wired from working into the late evening, she tosses and turns for an hour or more.

Bruno gets in around 9:00 a.m. the next morning, and checks his email. He sees the response from Karen, and sees that it's a long one. But he has no time to read it then, as he's already late for a 9:00 a.m. meeting. The message waits until 10:30 a.m. And so the saga continues. Over the next two days, the sequence of soliloquies bounces back and forth, carefully addressing points of contention and attempting to summarize what looks to be a very large project. Each response requires time to type and time to wait. Days pass. And both Karen and Bruno remark to their spouses how they don't know where the time goes. They say there's just too much to do and that they'll have to spend part of the weekend, probably Sunday, catching up.

Meanwhile, over in a different department of the same company, a different manager, Lisa, decides she needs to talk to one of her own people, Vern, about their own Spring campaign. Lisa picks up her phone and calls Vern. Seeing that it's his boss on the phone, Vern picks up. Lisa's tone conveys her need to talk about this spring issue; it carries layers of urgency and empathy that resonate well with Vern.

It pleases him that his manager, as busy as she is, recognizes the work he is putting into their various projects, and her acknowledgement feels good. She says she needs to talk to him this afternoon and would he be available sometime in the next half hour.

Vern says, "Let me finish my train of thought on this other project, and I'll come to see you in exactly 10 minutes." Lisa has always liked Vern's exactness with regard to time and knows he will be true to his promise to arrive in exactly 10 minutes. Since she knows exactly how much time she has, she takes the opportunity to return a couple of matter-of-fact emails confirming upcoming travel arrangements.

Ten minutes later, Vern arrives at her office. They discuss the spring campaign for 20 minutes. Taking subtle cues from eye contact, body language, and vocal tone, they are able to address the more contentious issues and arrive at an action plan that is workable and mutually pleasing. In fact, they enjoy a five-way communication structure:

1. Vern hears and sees what Lisa says, through her words, gestures, and body language.
2. Lisa hears and sees what Vern says, through his own words, gestures, and body language.
3. Vern hears himself as he speaks and is able to correct and refine his ideas on the fly.
4. Lisa is able to do the same as she hears herself speak.
5. Together they review their whiteboard writings, which, although messy, outline a strategy that will lead to the successful roll-out of the campaign. For safety's sake, Lisa takes a digital picture of the whiteboard. She will email it to Vern later as confirmation of their ideas.

The total time spent from initial phone call to conclusion: 30 minutes.

The silo that Bruno and Karen find themselves in is a creativity silo, based on the misconception that speed is the optimum answer for issues requiring human creativity. Further, the fear of the loop makes them think that all communications must be done via email in order that they become part of the "paper trail" or "audit trail," a concern otherwise known as the "CYA (Cover Your Assets) Factor."

The dividend that Vern and Lisa enjoy is obvious: greater productivity, shortened timelines, heightened understanding, and reduced stress. They incorporate the CYA factor only at the end, as a confirmation and summary of their mutual creativity.

Let's suggest, realistically, that the exercise that Vern and Lisa went through saved them just 50 minutes each (they probably saved more than that). Later, we'll return to this number and see what those 50 minutes saved can now do for them.

CANDID REACTIONISM

This chapter has attempted to demonstrate some of the larger scale costs of living and working at high speed. It proposes that a solution can be found through slowing down, or *cooling down* enough to inject a greater amount of person-to-person communication, which leads to greater control, vision, understanding, and productivity in the human-work relationship. Later chapters will deliver additional concrete examples of how to incorporate this into your life, but let's close this chapter by observing how high-speed results in one final form of theft, caused by candid reactionism. This can be illustrated using two different scenarios: the first, being robbed in a train station and the second, attending meetings.

Robbery through Reactionism

For the professional pickpocket, one of the best tools he could invest in is a wall-mounted sign that reads "Beware of Pickpockets." With this unlikely device, he needs simply to hang this sign on the wall of a railway or bus station and then sit back and observe as legions of well-meaning people casually pat their pockets or purses, reassuring themselves that their valuables are where they should be, all the while giving the thief clear instructions on where to find the goods.

This is because reaction, especially when done in self-defense, is quick, candid and innocent. By its very nature, reaction happens when a living being responds to a stimulus in an attempt to maintain the stability of its situation. When we react, we are not seeking to control a situation but merely to protect our existence within that situation. If, by contrast, you seek to control or change that situation, especially when it's to your benefit, then you are no longer reacting. You are pro-acting.

Hopefully, you might never get robbed by a pickpocket. But do you attend meetings? Do you meet with other people one on one, in groups, or on the phone? If you do, the same type of theft may be taking place.

When a meeting is called, the top priority often becomes the identification of the earliest date and time in which all team members (as well as a suitable room) are available. Assuming, then, that all people involved have agreed upon the meeting's necessity, who needs to attend, and the duration of the meeting, the event is then calendared and mentally shunted aside since there is too much else for everyone involved to do in the interim—too many other meetings, messages, and crises. When the time for the meeting rolls around, people arrive, perhaps on time, perhaps late. They receive the agenda, read through it, and slowly warm up their minds to the issues at hand. The odds are that such a meeting will be okay but will likely not meet the productivity potential (and cost) of all those people in attendance.

A chairperson's primary obligation is to recognize that all the people around a meeting table are expensive and that the chief objective of the meeting is to produce something that will justify the cost of these people. No matter what their hourly fee, whether it's $20 or $250, if people are sitting around a meeting table, they're not doing their other work, so, in fact, whatever their hourly rate, it's going to cost the company twice that (the cost of them being at the table plus the cost of what else they're not doing). As a result, it would be desirable to have all of these expensive people producing something that has a value greater than the double cost of their bottoms on the chairs.

Now, if we took all of these people around the table and morphed them, metaphorically, into one athlete, let's say an NBA player or an Olympic swimmer, it would be foolish to ask this player to hit the court or the pool without warming up first. Muscles might tear, ligaments might snap if we were to skip the tedious, slow ritual of stretching and warm-up. Yet in many organizations, meetings just start when they start and proceed as best they can, partly because we're too busy—there's too much to do during the week to strategize beyond the immediate.

But what if we were to *cool down* a little and take some time to ensure the meeting actually pays for itself? For example:

- What if the chairperson were to prepare and distribute the meeting agenda (an agenda that identifies the topics that are to be discussed, and therefore what is not to be discussed) a full day or more before the meeting? What might that do to help warm up the mental muscles? How much more productive might a meeting be if the attendees had had time to mull over these issues, even subconsciously, for a time, rather than reading them for the first time upon sitting down at the meeting table?
- What if the meeting chairperson were to choose who should attend, and who need not attend, and perhaps even position certain personality types at select places around the table (through the use of name tent cards), so as to dilute the potential for disruptive behavior or power cliques?
- What if the invitees were reminded and encouraged to slow down enough to actually read the agenda a full 24 hours prior to the meeting in order to capitalize on the warm-up described above and to re-instill in them the sense of importance surrounding the event?
- Similarly, what if we were able to create a culture where consecutive meetings were never scheduled back to back to always allow time for travel and recuperation between each, so that people arrived more prepared, more relaxed, and already mentally tuned in to the objectives of this event?

Such approaches aren't just feel-good practices any more than stretching and warm-up are for an athlete. That's not what they're for. They're there to bring about progress, profit, and success. Careful planning and production of a meeting also allows for more subtle, cerebral leadership skills to work their magic; ones that otherwise might get lost in the rush. Skills such as:

- Recognizing that just getting through a meeting's agenda does not constitute a successful meeting. A shrewd chairperson listens to what is being said *and* to what is not being said; she takes note of eye contact, body language, subtle and not-so-subtle gestures, and steers the meeting accordingly.

- Allowing silence for reflection, in order to allow ideas to percolate and to counter the actions of aggressive or domineering speakers. Silence is a scary concept for speed-oriented professionals. The desire to fill the air with words seems to soothe the high-speed mind by providing it with evidence of apparent progress—not always accurate evidence. This is a term that I call *ambient momentum*, and it will crop up again in a different situation in the next chapter. Silence, by contrast, allows creative thought to crystallize and grow. For example, a chairperson should be sure to count to seven after asking if anyone has questions or comments. Seven seconds is a painfully long time to spend staring at the faces of people around a table or in an audience. But that's how long the average person needs to both think of something to ask and to marshal the courage and/or energy to ask it.

- Factoring in time for the preparation of minutes. This overlooked and seemingly tedious part of the meeting process is essential to its ultimate success. Since the candid, reactionary nature of modern business forces all people, including the chairperson, to think "event to event," it is easy to envision a meeting that is scheduled to end at 2:00 p.m. to run the full length of that time, possibly more, after which everyone scurries off to their next appointment. By contrast, a chairperson who schedules an extra 15 minutes for herself and the minute-taker after the meeting has concluded to go over the minutes together, to keep them short, clear, and accurate, stands a better chance of seeing the meeting's action items actually come to fruition.

Do we have the right to such luxuries? To take the time to plan meetings, to browse the agendas beforehand, and to allow time for follow-up? Yes. Both a right and an obligation. We must push through the dust cloud that the culture of speed has thrown up and recognize that far from being luxuries, these techniques represent a realistic follow-through and prioritization of the workload. When we don't *cool down* and prepare for meetings, they run longer and are less focused, resulting in reduced productivity and greater overall expense—just as it is with so many areas of life.

Though this chapter has used meetings and email as primary illustrations of the Silo Effect, the concept goes far beyond just these at-work scenarios It applies to the way we plan projects, the way we do homework, and the way we make purchases. It impacts greatly the life of professional relationships, such as between a manager and her employee, or a supplier and a client. There is a great temptation, for example, to hide behind email during situations of conflict, discomfort, or when we are just pressed for time, and to leave voice mails when a discussion would be more appropriate. Ultimately such shortcuts diminish the skills of clear communication that professionals of all stripes need to draw upon if they are to keep up.

KEY POINTS TO TAKE AWAY

- Michael Eisner identified how technology is starting to erode the ability to understand human contact.
- The Silo Factor happens as a result of speed and results in significant intellectual isolation.
- Information Overload can lead to *infomania*, which results in lost productivity.
- We have a professional obligation to slow down and weigh the cost of immediate response against its benefits.
- The cost must be viewed in terms of all client relationships, not just specific ones.
- The need to stay in the loop is another human obsession based on a fear of being left out or of losing out.
- *Presenteeism* refers to people who expect to be able to work even though they are fatigued, ill, overstressed, or distracted.
- *Intellectual isolation* refers to the danger of ignoring or losing the sentient components of human communication, such as body language and speech rhythms. Teleconferences and videoconferences are somewhat less efficient for this reason.
- Pickpockets can teach us the value of not falling into reactive mode and being proactive whenever possible.
- The Tachometer represents the idea that people's mental state of energy and alertness is not always where we think it will be. If we had actual tachometers on our foreheads to measure our effectiveness, our awareness of the cost of speed and the value of *slow* would be much easier to accept.
- Meetings are a day-to-day example where speed and event-to-event thinking diminish the productivity of the meeting itself.

HOW TO *COOL DOWN*: THE SILO EFFECT
Putting Email Aside

Though email is an essential tool of business, it comes with a false illusion of priority.

- How possible might it be for you to close down your email for an hour? Or two? Or two separate hours in the day?
- What benefits in productivity might this deliver to you?
- What dangers might this pose?
- What might the reaction be from colleagues?
- What might the reaction be from your clients or customers?
- What might the reaction be from your boss?
- How might you sell this idea to these different types of people?

Responding to Email After Hours

- Have you felt the need to respond to a client after hours?
- Have you ever stopped to consider the deeper implications of doing this? What message do you think it sends to the client?
- Have you ever asked your clients about the perception it gives them of you?

Consider the types of communications you send by email each day. How many of them might have come to a quicker resolution if a phone conversation had been arranged instead?

Staying in the Loop

- A wireless PDA can actually be turned off. Are you willing to turn yours off? Why/why not?
- By succumbing to the temptation to read and respond to messages far outside of work hours, you will be conditioning others to expect the same behavior consistently and forever. How does this sit with you?

- Would it be possible for you to establish parameters for the times that you are available and not available to communicate, and to discuss these parameters with the people who need to know (clients, managers, etc.), being sure to reinforce in their minds the value this will bring to them in terms of having your undivided attention?
- How much do you fear being left out of the loop?
- What might happen if you were to take a day off from work? Do you have any fears about what you might miss?
- How about a week's vacation?
- What can you take from your fear statements above that might help eliminate your fears? Who might you talk to about them? What would you say?

The Sound of Silence

- How often do you reach for a phone or PDA when silence or downtime hits?
- Is this the best use of your downtime?
- If you didn't have any of these tools, not even change for a payphone, what would you do?

Human-to-Human Communication

- What is your own preference for communicating with others? Do you prefer email, voice mail, live phone conversations, or face-to-face meetings?
- Why do you prefer one over the other?
- Why do you think that is?
- What fears or reservations (if any) would you have if it were suggested that you deal with most work issues face to face from now on?

Escalation Issues

- Have you ever experienced a situation where a client called your boss because you did not answer promptly enough?
- What were the repercussions?
- What could you do to deal with escalation in the future?

Fire Your Weakest Client

There is an old adage taken from the 80/20 rulebook that suggests that people in sales should regularly review their client list and fire their "weakest client." The weakest client is the one whose demands and needs outweigh the value of the business they bring in.

- Regardless whether you are in sales or not, how might this principle apply to you?
- What are the "weakest clients" in your world, e.g. tasks, colleagues, technologies, expectations?
- What could you do to rearrange your daily structure to eliminate or at least minimize your weakest clients?

Presenteeism

- Have you ever been at work at a time when you really should have been home? For example, when you were ill, jetlagged from a recent trip, or just mentally overloaded from too many projects?
- What are your reasons for coming in under these conditions?
- What did you achieve?
- Might there have been alternatives?
- What would your boss say if you were to ask him about strategies for reducing presenteeism in other employees as well as yourself?
- Have you ever called in sick when you weren't sick but were just too tired or stressed to work?
- Have you ever called in sick just to play hookey?

Meetings

- How well do your meetings run? Are they quick and efficient or long and drawn out?
- What systems do you have in place for quantifying the value and profitability of a meeting?
- What impact do you think you would have on running meetings more efficiently even if you aren't the chairperson?

The Tachometer

- How are your energy and concentration levels during the day?
- How capable/empowered are you to assign certain tasks to coincide with your strongest/weakest times?

1 Eisner, Michael. "You've Got E-Mail, So Use It Wisely." Remarks by Michael D. Eisner, chairman and CEO, the Walt Disney Co. at USC's 117th Commencement, Alumni Memorial Park, May 12, 2000. http://uscnews.usc.edu
2 Strayer, David L., Drews, Frank A., and Crouch, Dennis J., A Comparison of the Cell Phone Driver and the Drunk Driver, *Human Factors: The Journal of the Human Factors and Ergonomics Society*, June 2006.
3 Pink, Daniel H., *A Whole New Mind: Moving from the Information Age to the Conceptual Age*, Berkley Mass Market, February 2006.
4 Murphy, Cait. "Secrets of Greatness: How I Work," *Fortune Magazine*, http://money.cnn.com/2006/03/02/news/newsmakers/howiwork_fortune_032006/index.htm

WHEN ONE TRAVELS FAST,

TREES BESIDE THE ROAD BECOME

A WALL MADE OF LEAVES.

CHAPTER 3

PERSONAL BLUR

Time for a quick review. In Chapter 1, I highlighted how human nature forces us to constantly want to take in more and more information (Parkinson's Law), and how this "brilliant haze of light" leads to a point of finite productivity (The Law of Diminishing Returns). In Chapter 2, I illustrated how this high-speed appetite has resulted in a reduction of interpersonal communication (Intellectual Isolation) and of productivity (Presenteeism). The next issue that needs investigation is how speed has conditioned us individually into living within a type of "event-to-event" thinking, which leads to hasty decisions and a further loss of opportunity due to not perceiving all the necessary details before acting.

THE ILLUSION OF SPEED

In the 100 years or more since the development of the first horseless carriages, automotive power has risen from 12 horsepower (hp) inside a 1904 Duryea Phaeton to 250 hp for a modern family car, and much, much more for those Porsches mentioned in this book's introduction.

Progress is constant and astonishing. James Bond's beautiful Aston Martin DB5, for example, which was considered a super-car in 1962, can now easily be outpaced by a well-tuned Honda. But as speed has increased, so has it decreased.

Take traveling, for instance. Though the available horsepower in a typical family car has increased twentyfold, people are not able to travel twenty times faster. For although cars themselves are capable of a great deal more speed, they seldom get to exercise this ability on major streets and highways. This is due not to any physical fault of the car, but to congestion, caused most often by the poor driving habits of aggressive, speed-obsessed drivers and lane-hoppers.

In China, where the desire for personal advancement has itself taken a great leap forward, 30,000 new cars are being added to the streets of Beijing each month. That's 1,000 additional cars every single day.[1] The traffic jams are unbelievable, and though the traditional bicycle is now being usurped by upwardly mobile urban Chinese people, it is often still the fastest way around town.

Regardless of the country, this rush hour paradox—faster cars but slower traveling—is a classic example of what happens when people think *speed* rather than *efficiency*.

The *Cool* Approach to Commuting

A study, performed in 1999 by Donald A. Redelmeier and Robert J. Tibshirani, sought to identify whether aggressive lane-hoppers really benefited from constantly switching lanes when driving in congested traffic. The study was based on a principle they called *roadway illusion*, namely, "that the next lane on a congested roadway appears to be moving faster than the driver's current lane even if both lanes have the same average speed."[2] Their findings showed that unless there was an actual lane obstruction such as an accident, no lane is faster than any other during high-volume rush-hour traffic. It appears to a frustrated driver that the cars and trucks in the other lanes are moving more quickly, but this is because most observers only really take note of such vehicular injustices when they themselves are being passed, and they are not so likely to see them when their own lane temporarily becomes the faster one. In addition, cars that pass an observer tend to remain in the field of view (up ahead) longer than those that have been passed.

Furthermore, many other traffic studies have shown that the slowdowns and bunch-ups that are commonplace during rush hour are caused, more often than not, by erratic acceleration and braking patterns rather than actual accidents. One car picks up speed, for example, and then is forced to brake as the traffic ahead slows. The driver of the car behind then often tends to over-brake, in order to allow for additional stopping distance. This creates a ripple effect, which quickly extends many miles backwards through the traffic, creating the slowdowns that seem to have no cause.

Our own research into discovering the existence of a truly faster lane has led us to conclude that on a congested road, the best lane to remain in is the outside lane—the one everyone merges into and exits from. This is primarily because as soon as the other drivers merge in, they quickly switch to the middle or inside lanes, expecting them to be faster. So, even though the outside lane handles more cars, it quickly disperses them. As a result, the best advice for getting somewhere quickly and coolly in congested traffic is to aim for the slow lane, because it's the quickest.

EVENT-TO-EVENT THINKING

The above examples of the relationship between cars, speed, and traffic jams highlight, by extension, the high-speed mode of thinking that causes problems in other areas of life. Delays cause stress primarily because any stoppage becomes an impediment between where a person is and where he or she would rather be. Life has conditioned us into a mindset that runs "event to event" (think about the pause-less sequence of shows and commercials on TV, for example), without factoring in intermediary time. People plan their days and fill their agendas as if they knew (or hoped) they had access to the transporter room on the deck of Star Trek's *Enterprise*.

Consider what I said about meetings in the previous chapter. The problem is not only that they often run less than optimally but that they are often booked too closely together. This is because the people doing the planning as well as the participants are trapped into thinking "event to event" and "meeting to meeting." How many times have you had to deal with a schedule full of back-to-back meetings? How often have you attended a conference in which the second event starts late because the opening address ran over the scheduled time? People tend to schedule things according to the old notion that one event must follow another in close succession because gaps of wasted time are evil.

I'm going to challenge that.

Certainly gaps of *wasted* time are not what people want in a day. But gaps need not be wasteful; in fact, they can make the difference between a reasonably productive day and a fully productive day. Meetings, activities, or events that run back to back, for example, are physically and mentally exhausting. Late starts impact the quality of the information to be delivered, and late wrap-ups impact subsequent events. Often it is the breaks that are sacrificed, which further threatens the success of the entire occasion. Such difficult days offer no opportunity to regroup, refresh, and prepare, which results in participants whose mental tachometers end up distressingly low.

Techniques for Running a Successful Multi-Meeting Day

- Schedule realistic times between events. I suggest 20 minutes. Give people enough time to refresh, go to the bathroom, and check their email. They will pay you back by participating more thoroughly.
- Start events at times other than "on the hour." For example, event A could run from 9:00 a.m. to 10:00 a.m., with event B running from 10:20 a.m. to 11:20 a.m.
- Allow time for small talk and venting, if you feel this is needed.
- Use a tool such as a bell or tapping a pen on a glass, or dimming the lights to usher people back to their seats quickly.
- Seek out meeting rooms that have copious sources of natural light.

How many different types of event-to-event situations can you identify in your day? What about getting up in the morning and getting your family and yourself out of the house and on their way? How about your commute in, your morning meetings, your travel itinerary? How about back-to-back phone calls, or *ad hoc* requests for your time in an already busy day? There are so many situations in which we force ourselves into an event-to-event mindset, and as each task block butts up against the one before it, we start to suffocate intellectually and the blur thickens.

What Are You Doing for Lunch? Cubicle for One?

I'm always amazed at the number of people who tell me they work through lunch. It's easy to see why. There's so much to do. Parkinson's Law stands at the ready to ensure that no matter how much gets done, there will always be a reason to do more during this valuable time, and event-to-event thinking creates the expectation that work must continue, no matter what. Personal time is so easy to sacrifice. After all, what value could it possibly have compared to the pressure of getting more done? It is intangible and subjective and therefore easily becomes secondary to work in terms of its significance. Personal time is not as definite or as firm as a scheduled event such as a meeting or a conference call. Consequently, when you meet someone in the elevator or kitchenette carrying his lunch back to his desk, you think little of it. It's normal. *It's expected.*

It's hard to *cool down* and take lunch when it's perceived solely as a self-indulgent act. But what if individuals and teams could be educated towards the idea that slowing down and taking a few minutes away from work actually increased productivity during the afternoon? What if people were able to see how taking a break from work for just 15 or 20 minutes to eat a *healthy* lunch (not fast food), not only replenishes the body with vital nutrients for the afternoon but also gives the creative mind a chance to step away from the momentum of the tasks at hand and refocus and condense the energies required to deliver quality? That might mean something: the idea that *rest* actually pays off.

A short midday lunch break also bolsters the metabolism in two important ways:

First, it energizes the body against the dreaded mid-afternoon trough, a period that occurs roughly around 2:30 p.m. and lasts between 30 minutes and an hour. For nine out of every 10 people, tasks become harder at this time, the brain becomes a little sluggish, and the body becomes a little sleepy as it seeks to take a quick afternoon nap. This physical depression is due to our innate 12-hour echoing of the deep-sleep period that occurs at around 2:30 a.m., but it can be lessened substantially by eating the right types of foods at the right pace. That means taking lunch and snacking on healthy foods throughout the day.

Naps, by the way, are *not* a solution to productivity problems even though they're precisely what people think of when they first hear about the *Slow* movement. Though some studies have shown that the nervous system does need a break in the mid-afternoon, the general understanding is that actual sleep in the mid-afternoon simply robs the body of depth and quality rest later on when it comes to overnight sleep. Overnight sleep is a multi-hour trip through various levels of brainwave activity that starts when you first doze off and ideally continues uninterrupted for six or more hours. Napping merely takes some of that sequence away and places it in the middle of the afternoon, leaving less rest for the night, and reduced quality of rest overall. Many people who allow themselves breaks throughout the day, along with adequate nutrition and fluids, find they don't need a nap. The breaks and refreshment are enough.

Optimum Lunch/Snack Choices for Productive Afternoons

- Foods that balance protein and carbs include tuna or chicken sandwiches on whole wheat bread.
- Snacks that can be stored at your desk include crackers, dried fruit, canned fruit, juice boxes, rice cakes, cereal, granola bars, instant soups and pastas, and almonds.
- Lunch/snack items that can be stored in the lunchroom fridge include bagels, bread, bran muffins, yogurt, cottage cheese, fresh fruit, raw vegetables, cheese, milk, and salad greens.

Foods to Avoid

- Heavy foods laden with carbs, fats, and starch
- Potatoes, pasta, pizza, hamburgers, and fast food

This conscious choice of taking time to eat the right types of foods helps to level out the metabolism and thus maintain energy throughout the day, while simultaneously bolstering the immune system against colds and infection. This is profound. It has direct economic value: *By simply slowing down enough to eat a small lunch, and therefore minimizing the afternoon trough, each of your staff members or colleagues stands to gain one hour of extra productivity per day.* If you have eight people on your team, this simple technique will win you back one person-day each week. By assisting your people in fighting off colds and other infections, you also help to cut back on both absenteeism and presenteeism, adding hundreds of more fully productive person-hours per year.

If this intellectual argument in favor of lunch breaks away from the desk hasn't grabbed you thus far, how about some purely biological facts? Studies have shown that eating over the keyboard is a health hazard, pure and simple. It has been proven that a computer keyboard and mouse contain 100 times more bacteria on their surfaces, nooks, and crannies than a kitchen table, and 400 times more than a toilet seat.[3] Their surfaces are constantly touched, often by many people, either directly or indirectly (think about shaking hands with someone and then returning to your computer). Germs and other nasty things can survive for hours, sometimes days, on dry surfaces such as computer equipment. Consequently, an employee might be able to squeeze 15 minutes more out of the day by working through her lunch, taking a bite of her sandwich, then working a little on her computer, then taking another bite, but when she then has to spend the next few days sick at home, or sick at work, her forehead tachometer will drop and stay dropped for a long time. And once the tachometer drops below 50 percent, all tasks, from the simplest phone calls to the most challenging knowledge work will take at least twice as long.

Speaking of Washrooms ...

The same goes for bathroom breaks. We need only recall the economic impact that disease outbreaks such as SARS and influenza had, and still have, on business. These illnesses are transmitted through contact with surfaces of all kinds. Following the SARS outbreak, a great number of organizations worldwide took the initiative and posted hand-washing instructions on the walls and mirrors of washrooms. The problem is, if people do not feel they have time to follow the posted procedures, the signs are pointless. The urgency of speed follows an employee right to the washroom basin. People who have to work too fast and think too fast will inevitably wash their hands too fast (far more quickly than the 15 seconds recommended by health authorities). And although that may seem like a personal thing, when it's your people who do this, who then interact with other people and with common tools and areas of the office, physical contamination will spread with the same efficiency and rapidity as a computer virus. Many companies have already calculated the financial cost of network-borne viruses to their IT infrastructure. But what will it take for them to create an environment in which human beings are afforded the same opportunity for health and safety? It's not soap and water that's missing; it's the attitude.

We did some analysis to see if this whole washroom thing was actually a real problem. We chose four companies at random, and posted an interviewer outside the door of selected staff washrooms (both men's and women's) at random times of the day. We asked the following simple questions:

a) Did you wash your hands?
b) If yes, how long did you wash them for?
c) Did you use paper towel or a heat dryer to dry them?
d) Which hand did you use to open the bathroom door upon exiting?

The results were interesting to say the least. Although most participants, 83%, said they washed their hands, few did so for 15 seconds with lathered soap. When asked why, the answer was "not enough time."

The reason for the fourth question—the one about which hand they used to open the door—is because regardless of the amount of time any individual spends washing his hands, once he touches the taps to turn them off and then grasps the inside door handle of the washroom in order to leave, he re-infects himself with the traces of all those who used the facilities before him.

This, then, is an example of how speed eventually reduces productivity, in this case through illness caused by insufficient hygiene. Busy individuals tend to neglect proper and complete hygiene procedures due to lack of time. Their minds are preoccupied with work, and therefore they don't take the time to consider the importance of this simple task.

What Are You Doing for Lunch? 100 M.P.H.?

Hagerty Classic Insurance, a provider of classic car insurance, used data from the National Highway Traffic Safety Administration (NHTSA) to identify the 10 most dangerous foods to eat while driving, since up to that point this data was largely unavailable to insurance companies.[4] They discovered that two of the biggest offenders are chocolate and coffee. You're most likely to spill or burn yourself with coffee, and chocolate will most likely get you into a swerving situation, or worse. Chocolate is sticky, it gets onto the steering wheel, and even worse things happen when it falls into your lap and starts to melt. With chocolate it's not the eating that's dangerous, it's the cleaning up. The other eight members of Hagerty's top-10 list are: hot soup, tacos, chili, hamburgers, barbecued food, fried chicken, jelly-filled or cream-filled donuts, and soft drinks. None of these foods, with the possible exception of soup, are particularly healthy to begin with, and since cars were never designed to be steered with the knees, they are simply dangerous, as are all other foods that are eaten while driving. They negatively impact safety, productivity, alertness, and health.

But people need to get where they're going. And as long as we live and think "event to event," lunch on the road becomes like lunch over the keyboard—a space of negligible personal time that can be sacrificed in the name of keeping up. A preoccupied mind, combined with an overloaded schedule, conspire to eliminate our awareness of how things could be done better.

- Driving while eating robs the mind of its driving talents. The first to go are realistic, defensive assessments of braking distances, followed by acclimatizing to changing road surfaces or obstacles (particularly in construction zones).
- Driving while eating further robs drivers of the ability to anticipate other drivers' actions. Reading a driver's body language can help predict fast lane changes, for example, or can help assess the safety of intersections in which other people are turning in front of you or running yellow and red lights.
- Food never stays where it's supposed to when you eat and drive. Even the easiest foods to eat tend to spill or crumble, often landing in hard-to-reach places.
- When it comes to hygiene, a steering wheel is just like a keyboard with regard to retaining and spreading germs.
- The final major danger of eating while driving has to do with food stains. They do nothing to enhance a positive image and can be a great source of stress.

I have spoken to many a road warrior who has learned, sometimes the hard way, that there is greater value in pulling over for 10 minutes to grab some lunch, rather than eating on the fly. Here are some of the comments they shared with me:

- "I find I eat slower if I stop driving. Then I don't get heartburn in the afternoon."
- "I don't get so hungry so quickly if I eat slower and stop driving. It's helped me lose weight."
- "It really cuts down on highway hypnosis."
- "I get a chance to check my schedule. If I can call people and tell them what time they can expect me, then there's less waiting around for me. I can actually see more of my customers by calling them just after I eat my lunch."
- "Sometimes I have to give my client a lift. Sometimes even my boss. It's really embarrassing to invite someone into your car when all of

the lunch stuff is still there. When I stop to eat, I can also make sure my car is presentable. That means a lot in my business."

- "It's just nice to get away for a while. I'm in my car, with my music on, or sometimes a book on CD. It just feels good."

Later I asked the person who made the fourth statement above, what would happen if he realized his schedule was too tight and that he couldn't make all his appointments that day.

He answered, "That has happened to me, and it's not a problem. My customers like to know that I'm looking out for them. If I tell one that I can't see him today, but that I will be able to come by tomorrow, he's fine with that. He's busy, I'm busy, and we know that. He's actually grateful for the call. It shows that I respect him."

This is a great example of how "high touch" wins out over "high speed." The customer is happy. He feels looked after. The road warrior is happy. He feels in control. His health is better since he has eaten slowly and carefully, and he will be in a better position to drive safely and still make his other commitments in the afternoon.

HIGH-SPEED AT THE CUBICLE FARM

Consider for a moment the deathbed anguishes of Robert Probst. As a designer, working for office furniture giant Herman Miller in the 1960s, Probst came up with the modular, three-walled work area that we now know as the cubicle. Seeking to create a high-productivity space for commercial innovation, Probst conceived the "Action Office," whose surfaces, both horizontal and vertical, allowed for clear thought, freedom of movement, ample storage, and the ability to lay out plans and drawings (there were no personal computers back then), all in a semi-open, semi-private configuration. Sadly, as is the fate of many creative architects, he watched as his modular workplace morphed into an economic convenience for the companies for which they worked, in which creative space gave way to an ice-cube tray-like formation, and the priority shifted away from ergonomic needs to economic ones. As *Fortune* writer Julie Schlosser puts it, the cubicle "still claims the largest share of office furniture sales—$3 billion or so a year—and has outlived every "office of the future" meant to replace it."[5] There are at least two ways in which the modern cubicle existence has contributed to the issue of lost productivity through speed.

Ambient Momentum

First is the idea of *ambient momentum*. The open-concept environment created by the cubicle provides sight barriers in three out of four directions, but it does nothing to lessen the distraction factor of ambient noise and activity. The atmosphere of the typical workplace delivers a host of distractions: conversations, phone calls, drop-in visitors, laughter, food aromas, mumblings, rustlings, arguments, gossip, and general busy-ness in a pretty constant fashion. There are some who can tune out this assault, but many cannot. Alongside distraction, which is costly enough, this activity creates its own momentum, a counterproductive speed of thought and action. When a person absorbs this ambient momentum, simply by sharing the same physical space, he ramps up to a higher, more frenetic level of thought and reaction without reaping similar levels of productivity or focus.

Ambient momentum, then, refers not to workplace noise itself but to the constant awareness of speed in the background, a subliminal presence that urges people on, beyond the pace at which the mind works best. The existence of ambient momentum is best proven by looking at the primary perk given to executives upon promotion: a corner office with a nice view and a closeable door—a refuge. Nothing contributes more to creativity and productivity than isolation and focus. It is a prize, a reward.

Examples of ambient momentum exist everywhere. Observe, for example, people's acceptance that meetings and events must be held back to back. In other words, the event-to-event mindset is nurtured by ambient momentum. So, too, is the act of over-booking schedules and over-committing to tasks. People who drive too fast are carrying over ambient momentum from the office. People who have trouble getting to sleep at night are taking ambient momentum to bed with them. Ways to combat ambient momentum are highlighted in the box on the following page, and are implicit in all of the other descriptions and solutions within this book. The idea is to understand that although ambient momentum can be disorienting, which does nothing for productivity or stress management, it can be controlled, quite simply, by *cooling down*.

Techniques to Combat Ambient Momentum

- Find an unused office or boardroom and "hide" there for an hour with your work. Leave a note letting people know when you'll be back.
- Go to a coffee shop and work there. The noise of other people's conversations will be less distracting due to their irrelevance.
- If you can only work at your desk, invest in a pair of noise reduction headphones (approximately $200). These help reduce ambient noise and tend to dissuade people from disturbing you.
- Position yourself away from direct sightlines of passersby. Avoid the temptation of looking at people during your period of focus. Use your body language to create a "shell."

Erosion of Human Contact

The second danger of cubicle existence has to do with its isolationism—the very thing Robert Probst sought to eliminate. The irony here is that although the cubicle grid structure of the typical office allows many people to work closely together, it has done little to improve actual human-to-human contact skills. People feel more comfortable hiding behind email than they do talking issues through, face to face, in a well-structured, dynamic discussion.

One example of this erosion can be seen in the case study of Karen and Vern in the previous chapter, who were unaware that an option other than email ping-pong was possible. It wasn't that they'd never heard of face-to-face meetings. Of course they had. But ambient momentum blurred such alternatives and made them invisible. Let's now consider some other examples. How would you deal with these situations?

- An accountant is busy preparing a client's tax return. There is some bad news about the return that is going to cost the client more money than she'd expected. The accountant procrastinates, agonizing for days over the phone call he'll have to make. He doesn't want to deliver bad news, and he doesn't know how to do it.
- A customer sends an email message inquiring about how to return a defective product to the company. The employee at the company sends back a standard email response he'd created just for this purpose. Too rushed to proofread the letter, he sends it with the wrong date, customer name, and product name on it. Distracted by a manager dropping by his cubicle wanting to chat, he forgets to schedule a follow-up call.
- An office employee is beginning to dislike a co-worker for her lax attitude towards punctuality on the projects she's been assigned. She puts her thoughts into a vindictive email and sends it to their mutual manager.
- A junior in a professional services firm gets exasperated by the fact that the senior partner keeps sending tasks for her to do by email, even though they work side by side. The junior recognizes that additional tasks are part of the job, but she feels that her senior is unaware of her current workload and unappreciative of her efforts and initiative.

These are examples of opportunities for interpersonal contact that have been eroded due to ambient momentum and the walls of the cubicle environment. In all of the cases above, solutions or resolutions could have been found and resolved faster if the people involved had known a little more about the value of human connection within the business process.

- The accountant, for example, could recognize that he need not be solely the bearer of bad news, but that he could apply his expertise to become part of the solution. With only a little courage he could guide his client through her short-term challenges and stay with her as a regular, reliable, and recommended supplier of business. She, in turn, would stay with him as a loyal client and a possible source of referral business.

- The employee who sent out the standardized, yet incorrect, email response could have increased his sales and won over the dissatisfied client by taking the time to talk to her on the phone, to agree with her complaints, and to demonstrate his acknowledgement of her distress as the first step in resolving the situation to her liking.
- The office employee who dislikes her colleague's lax behavior might do better to visit and talk with her, perhaps in the company of a third person as mediator, in order to learn more about where she's really coming from. Perhaps there are circumstances beyond the office walls that are contributing to this person's conduct.
- The final example highlights the disconnect that often happens between members of a closely knit team when clear communication and mutual understanding get shunted aside. The junior partner's talents are going wasted due to confusion, frustration, and anonymity. By working together, the two of them should be able to exceed the sum of their individual contributions.

The stories above might appear to be isolated examples. But they are analogies for many hundreds of other types of situations in which people miss out on faster, more productive opportunities due to personal blur. It's as destructive to individual efficiency as intellectual isolation is to groups. By being consciously aware of its presence, you will be able to identify blur as a threat and then strategize how best to *cool down* in order to achieve your goals more quickly and efficiently.

Ambient Momentum and the Departure Lounge

To demonstrate, let's make a parable out of two travelers in an airport departure lounge. This again is a situation-specific scenario whose lessons extend to many other areas of life.

It's hard not to be caught up by the tension of travel. It's a rootless existence where people stand halfway between home and their new destination, unable to access either. They battle jetlag, fatigue, and exasperation, while having to keep their wits about them to avoid missing important announcements. It may seem that boredom or frustration is the theme of the airport departure lounge, not personal blur. But let's observe how, when the moment hits, it's the cool, clear thinker who wins out.

Two travelers, Frank and Ernest, are sitting in the departure lounge. The PA system announces that due to a last-minute equipment change, the plane for their flight has been changed to a smaller one, and hence the flight is oversold.

Frank succumbs to the urgency of the moment. He leaps up and joins the other passengers, who all storm the agent at the gate. They demand answers, they vent their frustrations, and they demand to know how this situation will be resolved.

Ernest, however, does not. He knows there's no need to rush over and join his irate traveling companions in line. There's a cooler, more effective way. He takes out his wireless PDA and goes online to the airline's website. There, isolated from the contagious confusion of the departure lounge, he rebooks his flight online, with no extra cost or inconvenience.

Having circumvented the chaos, Ernest takes advantage of the privacy that the departure lounge offers. He intentionally left his office an hour early in order to negotiate city traffic and airport security with ease. He arrived unstressed at the terminal and now proceeds to get an hour of focused work done.

Frank, the unseasoned traveler and caught in the vortex of speed, did not see any value in planning ahead. Instead, he worked to the absolute last minute at the office, grabbed a taxi, and paid the driver double to drive as fast as possible. He saw no point in arriving early just to sit in an airport. And now the vortex continues. He still hasn't got a flight, and his blood pressure is dangerously high.

Ernest, on the other hand, works away on his laptop until his new flight is called. He takes his time, and strides toward the gate.

Which person would you rather be? Which one of these people reflects your current approach to crisis?

What can we learn from these cases? When people are forced, through the stress of speed and momentum, to gloss over the parts that complete the process, relationships remain incomplete and success becomes elusive. Such is the price of personal blur.

We've now spent enough time looking at damage. In the next chapter, we'll pause and see how situations like Frank's above gave rise to the actual global *Slow* movement. After that we will be in a better and cooler position to observe how we can accept and practice the techniques espoused by this movement in our busy lives.

KEY POINTS TO TAKE AWAY

- Although cars are physically capable of traveling faster, poor driving habits, fueled by an expectation of speed, cause wasteful delay.
- *Event-to-event thinking* forces people to act without factoring in necessary intermediary time.
- When planned for, gaps of time are opportunities for rest and creativity.
- The benefits of cooling and slowing down go far beyond the immediate and affect the quality of subsequent work, as well as the way you sleep at night.
- People who work through lunch do not gain as much as those who take a break, away from their desk.
- People who eat lunch while driving not only run the risk of being involved in an accident; they get no chance to mentally regroup and prepare for upcoming activities.
- *Ambient momentum* refers to noise and other activity within an open-concept environment that subconsciously drives people into a high-speed mindset.
- *Ambient momentum* also contributes to the decline in the human ability to communicate and resolve problems face to face.

HOW TO *COOL DOWN*: TIPS FOR AVOIDING PERSONAL BLUR

Blur

- Take stock of your day. Observe the moments when blur happens the most.
- Describe to yourself the cost of blur. Is it making you productive or is it ensuring you just tread water?

Lunch

- How often do you skip lunch?
- How often do you work through lunch?
- How often do you have "working lunches," or meetings in which lunch is brought in?
- Would you be able to schedule at least 15 minutes a day for lunch away from your desk?
- How would you alleviate your colleagues' worry about "losing" you during this time?
- Make sure your lunch includes time away from your desk, as well as a few minutes outside, for a change of air, light, and scenery.

Choosing What to Eat

- Do you feel you choose your at-work foods wisely?
- Do you tend to eat small amounts throughout the day, or just a single lunch at lunchtime?

The Dieticians of Canada Association Suggests

- To store at your desk: crackers, dried fruit, canned fruit, juice boxes, rice cakes, cereal, granola bars, instant soups and pastas, peanut butter, canned fish
- To store in the lunchroom fridge: bagels, bread, bran muffins,

yoghurt, cottage cheese, fresh fruit, raw vegetables, cheese, milk, salad greens
- To eat while on the road (after pulling over to a safe place): baby carrots, celery sticks, bagel bits, rice cakes, apples, crackers, pretzels

The 11:00 A.M. Snack

- At the very least, try snacking on low-fat yogurt around 11:00 a.m. and see how that affects your hunger an hour later. Most people notice that they feel less ravenous and are then able to choose a better lunch and to eat it less quickly.

Immediacy and Blur: Recognize That There Is Always an Afterwards

- Try to avoid getting caught up in the heat of the moment. When a large pizza or cheeseburger seems to be the most desirable choice for lunch, try to avoid succumbing to the temptation and look for better alternatives. All foods have the capacity to make you feel pleasantly full in about 20 minutes, so why not go for something healthier?
- If a high-stress situation occurs, remember there will be an "afterwards" to that, too. Knee-jerk reactions may not take you exactly where you want to go.
- Note your victories over personal blur in a diary. Don't let them die unrecorded.

Driving and Blur

- Perform the Outside lane test for yourself. Next time you find yourself in busy highway traffic, look for a unique vehicle that is near you but in a different lane, perhaps a yellow truck or a tour bus, and use it as a marker. Observe which of you gets through the jam first. Odds are good that you, in the outside lane, will win four times out of five.

Pulling Over to Eat

- A lot of people resist the desire to pull over somewhere to eat. Their initial reaction is to keep going. Is this you? Why is it so hard to want to stop and eat? Picture yourself enjoying a few minutes of quiet, of privacy of time to yourself as you eat you lunch, even if it is in the driver's seat of your car. Wouldn't it add more to your day than 15 minutes more of rushing?

Meetings and Blur

Could you influence the timing of meetings or your arrival and departure?

- What would this imply?
- Who might object?
- What might you say to them to sell them on the idea
- Who could you ask, e.g., a mentor who has been successful in scheduling well-paced meetings?

1 Friedman, *The World Is Flat.*
2 Redelmeier, D.A., and Tibshirani, R.J, "Why Cars in the Next Lane Seem to Go Faster." *Nature*, 401, p. 35.
3 Gerba, Charles P., PhD., "First in-Office Study Dishes the Dirt on Desks." Reported in *Market Wire*, April 15, 2002 http://www.marketwire.com/mw/release html b1?release_id=40596&category=
4 "The 10 Most Dangerous Foods to Eat While Driving." Quoted in Insurance. com___http://www.insurance.com/Article.aspx/The_10_Most_Dangerous_Foods_to_Eat_While_Driving/artid/140
5 Schlosser, Julie, "Cubicles: The Great Mistake." *Fortune Magazine* quoted in CNN   Money___http://money.cnn.com/2006/03/09/magazines/fortune/cubicle_howiwork_fortune/index.htm?cnn=yes

MANY BOOKS TEACH *SLOW*.

THE CHALLENGE: TO GET THROUGH THEM.

A SPEED-READING CLASS?

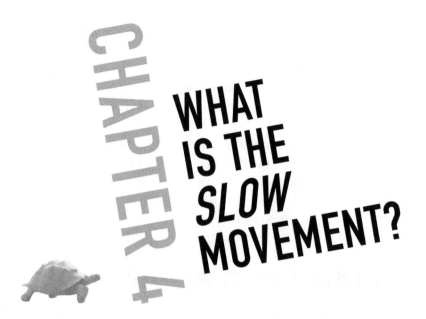

CHAPTER 4
WHAT IS THE SLOW MOVEMENT?

So, does the *Slow* movement hold the answer to our current and future productivity woes? Is it truly a social force to be reckoned with? Is it a legitimate tactic for refining a person's ambitions and skills, or is it merely a refuge for those who cannot handle the pace of business?

My belief is that the concepts behind the *Slow* movement do offer promise, but as long as they continue to run smack into the collective high-speed mentality of most North American business people, there will be no progress, and worse, no perceived need for its philosophy. The mindset that embraces speed and advancement has been fueled in the United States by over two centuries' worth of the pursuit of independence, progress, and personal freedom. Slightly younger countries (constitutionally speaking) such as Canada and Australia hold similar collective desires. Nor is the "old world" immune to the pressures of speed. Some companies and organizations in Spain, for example, have actually tried to eliminate the centuries-old tradition of *siesta,* replacing it, in some instances, with fast-food lunch vouchers in order to a) remain more accessible to the 24/7 marketplace and b) fit into the new commuting schedules of households with two working parents.

As the global economy continues to both advance and diversify, the pressure on working professionals to do more with fewer resources, to remain accountable to their worldwide customer base, while simultaneously staying ahead of their competitors, will only become more intense. The collective reaction to all this will be to want to hurry up, not slow down.

Negative stress that accompanies such pressure is what causes the damage, both for individuals and the companies for which they work. As I described in Chapter 1, it's the difference between walking fast because you like to and walking fast because you have to. When people or companies react and increase their pace because they have to, they move into the emotional territory where fear and anger live.

FEAR AND ANGER AS A REACTION TO PRESSURE

When a person feels fear, he experiences an increase in energy brought about by the release of adrenalin into the bloodstream. This also increases his blood pressure, and both together are intended to help him either avoid trouble or get out of its way quickly. However, these reactions are soon tempered by a separate branch of the autonomic nervous system called the parasympathetic system, which seeks to bring the state of hyper-arousal back down to more normal values. People are not built to stay in this heightened state for long periods, just as we're not built to sprint marathons every day. We just can't.

Anger, similarly, is a state of emotional intensity that usually comes about as a reaction to a negative situation. When a person is feeling anger, she may experience a similar sensation of emotional arousal, a surge of vitriolic passion, and a desire for instant action. But, in fact, in the face of the anger response, the heart's ability to pump blood efficiently through the body drops significantly, which puts certain people at risk for disturbances in heart rhythm (arrhythmias). It can also do significant damage to your lungs. Anger is not a healthy emotion.

It is interesting to note that the physical stresses brought on by fear and anger differ markedly from those brought on during another high-intensity situation: strenuous, enjoyable exercise. The reduction in blood-pumping efficiency does not happen during periods of *eustress* (positive stress). Exercise, though vigorous, is still a form of relaxation, akin to walking fast because you like to. The difference, in terms of experience between what the body feels when angry or fearful, compared to what it feels during times of enjoyment demonstrates the wide scope of physical and mental repercussions that must be understood if we are to live healthy and productive lives. No place better illustrates these repercussions than urban Japan.

KAROSHI

The *Slow* movement started in Japan in reaction to a very real problem known as *karoshi*, translated as "death by overwork." Real death, not just disillusionment or boredom. We're talking about hard-working professionals, in their 30s, 40s, or 50s with no obvious signs of illness who one day simply keel over. There are two primary causes of death through *karoshi*: the first is heart attack and the second is stroke. Both are brought on by a noxious mix of overwork, stress, and pressure.

Since the first official case in 1969, Japanese officials have tracked all cases of *karoshi*, primarily because of its grave implications for the Japanese workforce, but also, I would suggest, with an eye to the growing number of lawsuits being brought forth by grieving families of the deceased. The Japanese Ministry of Labor regularly publishes statistics on the spread of this affliction.

Japan was, and still is, a fertile breeding ground for *karoshi*. For decades, its work culture expected that no worker was to leave the office at the end of the day until everyone was finished, usually well after 8:00 p.m. An average of two hours of unpaid overtime per day was expected and was dutifully given. It was all about "face time." It was also expected that colleagues join each other for drinks after work where, within the tightly constrained cultural atmosphere of urban Japan, small talk, gossip, or criticism could be expressed and conveniently excused as "the alcohol doing the talking." Millions of exhausted Japanese businessmen, in later decades to be joined by exhausted businesswomen, would then squeeze themselves into packed commuter trains, returning home late in the evening to grab three or four hours' sleep before starting the ritual again. Japanese professionals who have kids routinely use the services of extended-hour daycare centers and overnight nanny services, but even the population of overworked parents is dwindling. Japan's birthrate is plummeting, and the cause is directly linked to overly long work hours.[1]

It's not as if the Japanese consciously desired to become workaholics and absentee parents. It was simply the result of a combination of elements, including tradition, economic expansion, ambition, and necessity. These created the circumstances for such an impossible workload to take root. For a while it seemed like a good thing. But there are some in Japan who have started to question this commitment to death-in-harness and have begun to express a desire for the adoption of a less hasty lifestyle. The answer, they believed, was to adopt and practice the principles of *Slow*.

The Japan Consumer Marketing Research Institute (JCMR) published, and continues to publish, a series of reports that shows how some of their country's consumers are indeed consciously shifting to a "slow life" consumer lifestyle. The JCMR, which advises national and international companies on trends and business opportunities in Japan, identifies, for example, how some Japanese males in their 40s and 60s are now leading the downshift into the "slow life" consumption pattern.

Certain towns have gone as far as to take revolutionary steps in aid of the *Slow* movement. The prefecture of Iwate, for example, located in northern Japan, re-elected its governor, Hiroya Masuda, in 2004 for a third term on a platform of "pro-relaxation" with 88 percent of the votes cast. Says Mr. Masuda:

> In Tokyo, people are chased by speed, and life consists of working, eating, and sleeping … Here, I want people to go home early in the evening, take a walk with their family, and talk to the neighbors.[2]

Iwate's achievements are interesting, and its coastal countryside is beautiful, but it remains to be seen whether the approach to *slow* adopted there has universal appeal. Much of the interest in the area, indeed much of the traffic into and out of Iwate, seems to come from stressed Tokyo-ites, eager for a rare weekend of rest and relaxation, but compelled to return to their own city's harried streets come Monday.

Kakegawa, further south, declared itself a "Slow Life City" in 2002. Located south of Tokyo, it aimed to become a city that promoted a comfortable lifestyle and relaxed state of mind, not only with regard to the pace of work and food, but also to "slow industry," in which competitive production was maintained with ecologically friendly approaches to industry and economic development. Kakegawa, like Iwate, is a beautiful place to visit but would you really want to live there? These are small, and not overly prosperous towns, after all. Do they represent the turning tide in terms of the global approach to *slow?* Perhaps not by themselves, but they have friends.

THE SLOW CITIES MOVEMENT

There are many other towns and small cities around the world that have joined with Iwate and Kakegawa to embrace the *Slow* movement. Together they form a collective, under the banner "Cittaslow" (pronounced chit-a-slow), a made-up pseudo Italian-English term meaning "slow city." The goal of Cittaslow is to draw global attention to towns and administrations that have undertaken steps to restore historical centers, boost the use of recyclable containers in public structures, promote the greening of private and public spaces, and encourage car-free zones. It's largely a European movement, and its website, www.cittaslow.net, is accessible in both English and Italian.

It would be very easy for those comfortable with the culture of speed and wary of change to dismiss the Cittaslow concept as rather provincial, even quaint, given that all of its founding cities are far from economic powerhouses. But therein truly lies the beauty of the *Slow* movement and its own sort of simplistic sophistication. More and more people are realizing that enduring the trade-off of having to work 80 hours a week simply to maintain a lifestyle within the boundaries of a major metropolitan area is no longer the only choice. They are discovering that there are other, less expensive, less demanding, more enjoyable ways to live.

Carl Honoré, author of the definitive summary of the *Slow* movement, entitled *In Praise of Slow*, highlights the simple math that often gets obscured by the fog of high-speed workaholism:

As it turns out, people who cut their work hours often take a smaller hit financially than they expect. That is because spending less time on the job means spending less money on the things that allow us to work: transport, parking, eating out, coffee, convenience, food, childcare, laundry, retail therapy. A smaller income also translates into a smaller tax bill … some workers who took a pay cut in return for shorter hours actually ended up with more money in the bank at the end of each month.[3]

Consequently, it makes sense for smaller towns to embrace the movement without fear. They have discovered an alternative richness to life, other than just money or corporate power, which more and more people are starting to see as both attractive and practical.

THE *SLOW FOOD* MOVEMENT

Perhaps the most famous of the *Slow* movements is the *Slow Food* movement, also an international organization, whose aim is "to protect the pleasures of the table from the homogenization of modern fast food and life."[4] Centered in Europe, and particularly active in France, the movement encourages not just the purchase of organic and locally grown foods, but also the pleasure of taking time to eat. The French have always been famous for their passion for rich and elaborate food, yet as Mireille Guiliano, CEO of the champagne company Veuve Clicquot, and author of *French Women Don't Get Fat: The Secret of Eating for Pleasure*, explains, there are better approaches to maintaining or losing weight than becoming obsessed with diets and deprivation. A lot, she says, simply has to do with eating right, exercising well, and enjoying life.

Okay, I'm sure there are a few overweight women and men lurking in the cafés of Paris and Nice, but much of the success of this philosophy has to do with a traditional approach to dining, a far less hurried one, that many people in France enjoy. They take the time to savor the meal, to review its presentation, to take note of its many flavors, and, while dining, they enjoy passionate conversations or arguments. They talk as well as eat. This gives their digestive systems more time to receive and process the food, without being forced to literally pack it away as body fat. In addition, a good intellectual discussion, even a satisfying argument, helps stimulate endorphins and other activators in the brain, setting the stage for a productive, alert afternoon, even after consuming a substantial meal with wine.

That's all very nice for all people over there. The French get to eat, the Italians get to walk across their city squares, and the Japanese get a chance not to die quite yet. But what does all of that have to do with people in North America and other speed-obsessed centers of business? Well, have a look again at a significant fact hidden within Mme Guiliano's description above. She mentions how her attitude to eating provides a better approach to weight loss than diets and deprivation do. What she demonstrates with that statement is that there are often better tactics than the merely obvious. When it comes to food, the obvious and expected approach for North Americans is to diet, which results in cravings, cheating, and shameful feelings. Diets seldom work for long since they go against the natural tendencies of the body, and in many cases the weight simply returns. But since dieting has been with us for decades now, it is accepted as the social norm. Mme Guiliano's approach, however, is to continue to eat, but to eat in a measured, slower way. This, she shows, achieves greater progress, a more stable, natural approach to weight management without cravings, and is also much easier.

So it is with *Cool Down*. The purpose of this book is not to repeat what Mr. Honoré and Mme Guiliano say in their books, but to show that the same unconventional approach that they so eloquently describe can be successfully implemented within the North American work culture. By doing things differently, rather than completely depriving yourself of them, alternatives appear. It would be foolish for example, to wrestle a wireless PDA away from its addicted owner. It would be dangerous, also, to suggest that no calls or emails should *ever* be answered after hours. These things are too close to the comfort level of busy professionals, and the withdrawal that they would feel would cause them to return to their current habits. That's not what *Cool Down* is about. Instead it's about revising those habits, to ensure that the trivial does not get pulled along with the truly important, and that conscious awareness of the value of every moment is constantly assessed and accounted for. Ultimately, this demonstrates that not only is *slow* an easier route, it is actually more effective and productive.

SAY IT AIN'T SLOW

One of the major liabilities of the *Slow* movement is the word itself. The word *slow* is anathema to the mentality of business upon which the North American economy professes to be built. The term triggers a bias; many view it as bad. It connotes unproductive activity, reduced energy, coming in second or third in competitions. Negative concepts spring quickly to mind, such as work-to-rule job action, or retirement (forced or otherwise), or of being old or old-fashioned. In the minds of ambitious people, *slow* paints a picture of uselessness, frustration, and a laid-back counterculture approach to life. It brings to mind images of traffic jams, of dot-matrix printers buzzing away, line by line, and of old people standing patiently in a queue at the bank to pay their phone bills. None of these has a strong appeal to ambitious inhabitants of the working world. But this again is because the term *slow* has, to this point, been framed mostly within the context of non-productivity.

However, there is another perspective. *Slow* can mean productive. It can also mean making money. More and more companies are seeking to redefine *slow*, to integrate it so as to be better aligned with healthy, profitable business practices, in which flexibility, balance, and life issues rank as highly as corporate ethics and transparency and product quality. Throughout this book, I profile successful executives who have discovered and implemented the power of *slow* in their own ways. There are many companies that have started to take the plunge.

Alcan

In 2003, Montreal-based aluminum producer Alcan Inc., in an attempt to stem the tide of high employee turnover due to burnout (people were working seven-day weeks, 13 or 14 hours a day), implemented a "work-life effectiveness strategy" that included mandatory no-work hours, as well as on-site experts in work-life balance. Alcan's executive had recognized that employee burnout posed a bigger long-term threat to its business than the short-term cost of encouraging staff to slow down.[5]

Since this book is about the nuts-and-bolts of how *Slow* might work within the context of business, I found the greatest significance of the Alcan story to be the commitment made by senior management, not merely to endorse the program, but also to act as role models. They have insisted their staff practice "no-work" weekends and out-of-office lunch breaks, and they then balance this out by urging employees to focus on "essential" rather than "important" tasks, to avoid working late.

AstraZeneca

On a recent visit to the Canadian head office of global pharmaceutical company AstraZeneca Inc., I was pleased to observe the extent to which workplace health had been so thoroughly incorporated into their community. Employees informed me that, yes, they were actually encouraged to use the extensive health and exercise facilities and that this was allowed even during the workday.

As Anna Blake, AstraZeneca's Manager of Employee Wellness, told me, "It's important to have an HR policy supporting Work-Life Balance. Employees have their core hours between 10 and three. Some start early or leave late, and they can also juggle around their lunch."

One of the unique and fascinating things about AstraZeneca's approach is the instructor-led exercise sessions. The instructors are volunteers—AstraZeneca employees—who have been trained to deliver the exercise classes. Anna pointed out, "There's a lot of companies who, when they talk about wellness they talk about having a committee. We think it's more important to get them actively involved in it." The "them" in this case referred not only to the main-line employees but the vice-presidents too, many of whom play on the company's hockey team.

AstraZeneca's multi-dimensional commitment to wellness covers more than just exercise; it also deals with social and psychological issues. In addition to the exercise facilities, they also offer cooking and watercolor classes. They even have their own art gallery to display their employees' creativity.

Companies and their senior executives are recognizing the difference between working full-out, and working smart. In a sense they are catching up to their computers. It has always intrigued me that for many of the companies I visit the most comfortable room in the workplace is the server room. It is usually air conditioned, clean, and always well looked after. It makes sense, after all, because that's where the computers live, and without them, the company could not run. Some organizations are now recognizing that the same standards can promote optimal human functioning. They have seen that although wireless technology allows employees to work from anywhere and at any time, this has not resulted in proportionate increases in productivity. Busy-ness does not equal business.

Carlos Ghosn, CEO of both Renault (France) and Nissan (Japan), was interviewed by *Fortune* magazine for the article *How I Work*. He describes the superhuman effort it takes to keep up with his workload, given that he has to travel to opposite sides of the world regularly each month. Yet with all that he has to do, he still points out the value of cooling down:

> It is also important to take a distance from the problem. I do not bring my work home. I play with my four children and spend time with my family on weekends. When I go to work on Monday, I can look at the problem with more distance. I come up with good ideas as a result of becoming stronger after being recharged.[6]

What a marvelous demonstration of the power of cooling down. Even with the pressure of running two companies half a world apart, Mr. Ghosn applies conscious control to maintain equilibrium between his work and his recuperation/family time. He demonstrates that far from being a passive act, cooling down is about actively creating perfect balance.

Remember Esperanto? Memori Esperanto?

Esperanto is a language that was designed to be the *lingua franca* of the world. Developed in 1880 or thereabouts by a Polish ophthalmologist, Dr. Ludovic Lazarus Zamenhof, it still exists, with an estimated 10,000 to 100,000 people using it regularly, mostly in Central Europe and parts of post-colonial Africa. It's not exactly heard regularly in coffee shops on Main Street in North America, but it's well known enough that you can order an Esperanto add-on for Microsoft Word.

The reason why Esperanto never really took off has more to do with one of its own greatest accomplishments: It is borderless and cultureless. It has no official status in any country, and it has no true roots within any group or society. It was invented out of a theoretical concept, and then introduced to a diverse group of peoples. When an organic thing such as a language has no roots, it stands little chance of growing. When it also lacks the opportunity to be nurtured, it has little chance of surviving. Esperanto still exists, in pockets here and there, but it will never be able to outpace the growth and continued natural evolution of languages that live and breathe. It is said, for example, that 50 years from now, the English language as it is spoken today will be very different, as words, terms, and tonality from other dominant languages become part of it. However, the roots of English will still be evident, just as the Germanic, Latin, Norse, French, and Sanskrit roots of today's English are still visible beneath the surface, and the language will continue to be used. It has a purpose and it has practicality.

This is how I see the problem facing the *Slow* movement. Business people in North America see *slow* as a kind of Esperanto term. Useful for someone else, and perhaps even useful here, but it is not in keeping with the culture of speed and progress. People find it hard to acknowledge the damage that high speed and long hours are doing to them. Some may be looking for an escape, but others believe the current pace is necessary for survival. So our challenge is to make the idea of slowing down sell itself, through practical tips and a demonstration of its payoff. Only then can the roots begin to take hold.

The first step, I believe is to refrain from calling this approach *slow*, and instead use the term *cool*. The word *cool* is one of the most popular terms in the Western world, and one that spans cultures and generations effortlessly. It evokes more positive feelings than does *slow*, and connotes a greater sense of control and achievement. The question now, is, should you embrace the *Slow* movement through cooling down? The following chapters aim to demonstrate practical ways in which doing so can improve and maybe even save your life.

KEY POINTS TO TAKE AWAY

- The concepts behind the *Slow* movement can work well, but they need to be explained in order to win over the current mindset of the North American business community.
- When countries or companies react impulsively and defensively to the pressure of a changing world economy, they start down the same destructive path as individuals who feel stress or anger.
- *Karoshi* refers to "death by overwork," and can be seen as a catalyst in the development of the *Slow* movement in Japan.
- *Cittaslow* is a collection of towns around the world that have embraced slow ideals. (www.cittaslow.net)
- The *Slow* Food movement encourages people to purchase organic, locally grown foods and reintroduces the pleasure of taking time to eat.
- One of the major liabilities of the *Slow* movement is the word itself, which is anathema to Western business.
- *Cool* is a better term since it connotes positive control.

HOW TO *COOL DOWN*: USING *SLOW* IN DAILY LIFE

The Term *Slow*

- What does *slow* mean to you?
- What does it mean to your manager?
- In what ways could you positively apply *slow* to your workplace?
- How might *slow* affect productivity and sales?
- What might *slow* add to your life?
- How could you redefine *slow* and sell it to your manager and other stakeholders?
- What might *slow* do to improve customer relationships, product quality, service, and accuracy?

The *Slow* Movement

- Visit www.cittaslow.net just to have a look.
- Visit www.slowmovement.com to have a look.
- Use the News Alert feature of Google to keep tabs on other companies (perhaps your competitors or customers) who are embracing principles of the *Slow* movement.
- For more information on the *Slow* movement itself, pick up a copy of *In Praise of Slow*, by Carl Honoré.

Eating

- How often do you get to take more than 20 minutes for lunch during a workday?
- Since it takes 20 minutes for your stomach to tell your brain to stop eating, how do you think a slightly longer lunch might affect your diet and health?
- What are you prepared to do to act on this?

Role Models

- Ask your friends and colleagues about their companies' use of *slow*.
- Do they have good or bad examples?
- How might these be used as part of your pitch?

Mentors

- Seek out a mentor who has practiced *slow* in his/her own business. Invite her to have a coffee with you. Learn what has worked for her and what has not.

1 "Japan's Long Work Hours Linked to Declining Birthrate, Government Says." *MainIchi Daily News*, October 10, 2006.
2 Moffett, Sebastian. "Unprosperous Japanese State, Egged on by Its Governor, Goes Slow and Likes It." *The Wall Street Journal*, June 30, 2004; Page A1.
3 Honoré, Carl. *In Praise of Slow*. Random House Vintage Canada (June 2004), p. 201.
4 Source: Slowfood.com
5 Gulli, Kathi. "All Work, No Play, No More: What Happens When a Company Orders Its Workers to Slow Down." *Macleans*, June 15, 2006.
6 Murphy, Cait. "Secrets of Greatness: How I Work." *Fortune Magazine*, http://money.cnn.com/2006/03/02/news/newsmakers/howiwork_fortune_032006/index.htm

WHEN THOUGHTS GET OBSCURED,

ANSWERS SUDDENLY APPEAR

IN THE SKY'S BLUE FACE.

CHAPTER 5
THE POWER OF THE BLUE SKY

To "blue-sky" means to stare out at the sky. Whether it is clear blue and featureless, whether there are clouds slowly passing by, or even if it is gray and overcast or black and starry, the sky offers a unique canvas upon which to rest your gaze. There is no need to focus hard, there are no distracting details, yet it's a visual scene of enormous potential.

The act of blue-skying is a powerful, creative intellectual undertaking. It allows the mind to work on problems, ideas, and opportunities that the busy-ness of the day-to-day tends to obscure. Blue-skying is one of the major benefits of *slow*, and therefore represents one of the major watersheds in any individual's destiny, since it is the act of blue-skying that allows people to do what needs to be done most: to continue to innovate and excel in a way that fosters ongoing growth and success. Some people have the time for this; most don't.

There is enormous value in taking your eyes away from work and focusing them on the sky, in the name of productivity, not of work avoidance. Leisure by itself is nice, and valuable, but the theme of this book is about using *slow* to get further ahead, which means, finding ways to advance, by taking time away from the momentum of "now," and applying it to the deeper possibilities of the future.

In Chapter 2, I described numerous examples and scenarios in which people feel the need to stay in the loop for fear of being left out. In Chapter 3, I introduced the term *ambient momentum* to highlight the atmosphere of speed that perpetuates the workplace and contributes to the fogging of creative, strategic thought. Blue-skying is the antithesis to both of these afflictions.

Take elevators, for example. A person who travels in an elevator "solo," that is to say not engaged in conversation with anyone else in the car, faces a full 45 seconds or so of idleness between the time he presses his floor button and the time of his arrival. He enters a void of inactivity: 45 seconds with no external stimulation. This is anathema to the speed-minded person. So he reaches quickly for his wireless PDA. What if he doesn't have one yet? No worry. He can instead check to see if his cell phone has reception. Failing that, he can read the elevator's own in-car television monitor to get the latest headlines, stock prices, and ads. Anything to fill that void. What this elevator passenger is doing is filling up on high-satisfaction, low-value intellectual stimuli. He's filling his mind up with the activity of busy-ness brought on by the ambient momentum of his high-speed life. Such activities satisfy a need, but do little for overall productivity.

A 45-second elevator ride is a perfect place to do what people used to do before wireless PDAs, cell phones, or elevator TV ever existed: stare at their shoes and think about something. Think about what? Well, whatever comes to mind. In Chapter 2, I mentioned the seven-second rule, which is useful during meetings to find out if anyone has a question or a comment. Seven seconds is a long time to wait, but that's how long it takes for people to process, question, and then summon the courage and energy to verbalize. It takes time for individual thoughts and ideas to realize that they might have a chance to step forward from the recesses of the brain and express themselves. Thoughts that might save time, create new opportunities, or generally do good things—they're all in there. But every time they try to make themselves known, they're brushed aside by another fast-moving "immediacy." These ideas find little opportunity to make themselves known in our busy world, and collectively we run the risk of losing them forever.

Physiologically, the reason blue-skying is called what it's called is because letting your eyes come to rest while they are open is actually quite difficult. The eye and the entire optical sensory system are programmed to move ceaselessly from object to object. Most people are unaware of just how many times per second their eyes move from one item to another, pulling in thousands upon thousands of bits of information to be processed and prioritized by the brain. It truly is fantastic. There are way too many distractions in a typical workplace for blue-skying to occur.

Blue-skying requires a visual panorama that can encompass the entire field of view, including your highly sensitive peripheral vision and that commands soft focus, not hard focus. An actual blue sky is the easiest and most obvious choice, but there are others:

- Moving water, as in a fountain, stream, or lake
- A sunset or sunrise (assuming you do not stare straight into it)
- A busy city street full of anonymous, walking people
- The steam rising from a cup of coffee or tea
- The act of staring out of the window of your train or bus, or even out of a car window (for all but the driver)

Tips for Helping You Choose to Blue-Sky Rather Than Read E-mail

- Remember that great ideas need a few seconds to "warm up and come forward."
- Remember that great ideas are fleeting. If they're not captured now, they may be lost forever.
- Remember that problems are best solved by mentally letting go of them.
- Remember that email can and will wait.
- Consider your blue-skying time to be on par with being in a meeting with a customer. Would you interrupt a conversation to take a call or read an email? (Hopefully not.)
- Remember your success is based on your ability to influence people. That comes from deep within.
- Remember that blue-skying also sets you on a path for healthy sleep, which is the single greatest ingredient for top productivity.
- Remember that the human body and mind need refreshment in order to work at peak.

A second form of blue-skying is also available when you create a soft-focus visual panorama through the physical preoccupation of the rest of the body: Jogging and swimming are good examples, and so are using an exercise bike or treadmill (so long as you do not read or watch TV while doing it). Outdoor cycling is not an effective blue-sky technique, since the eyes and mind need to be on constant lookout for danger.

It is probably obvious by now that one of the central tenets of this book is this: Slowing down long enough to stare at the sky presents greater benefit for personal success in both the short and long term than does attending to more immediate visual priorities. That's indeed the theme of this battle. People are hesitant to give themselves permission to blue-sky. It's alien to the event-to-event mentality they have been conditioned to accept. Getting permission to blue-sky is difficult enough when you have something to think about. But what if you do not know what blue-skying will bring you? How can you hope to justify it then? To those people I offer the image of a spider spinning a web. When a spider chooses a place to spin a web, the first line of web she produces does nothing. No creature will be caught by a single line of thread. The same applies for the second line she produces, and the third, and the next 100. At this point she has not created a structure strong enough to trap her next meal, just feeder lines that drift in the air currents until they find something solid to stick to. Should she continue? Yes. Although a quickly honed collection of strands will do nothing except exhaust her, it becomes the foundation for a full web that itself can only come about through slow, diligent effort. Yet for this spider, even when she has finished her web with its hundreds of strands and thousands of connections, she will still not be sure exactly what it might catch—what the next great "thing" will be. But she knows it will be something, because something always comes along. Thus it is with blue-skying. Sometimes the right thought pops up immediately. Sometimes, however, you have to let your mind get used to its new liberty; to get in shape, as it were for this newfound opportunity to be creative. Even when no profound thoughts appear, there will still be positive action happening below the surface: synapses connecting, patterns emerging, the thought process flourishing.

A PRESCRIPTION FOR TENNIS

Let me tell you a story: I was attending an event with a team of chartered accountants once, when I was approached by a student who was in the midst of studying for an exam that would count towards his professional qualifications. He was exhausted. He looked exhausted, he did not smile, and he did not even want to be at the convention. This is sad, because professional conventions can be (and should be) prime learning and networking opportunities. But because of the amount of studying he still had to do, all he was aware of while attending the event was the study time he was losing. This student asked me for any tips and tricks I might have for improving his study habits. He was falling asleep too much, he said, and the things he was studying were just not staying in his head.

I asked him what he used to do for fun. What sports or activities did he once enjoy? His answer was tennis, and I could tell it was true. For a brief second, his eyes lit up as he remembered his days on the court. So as a "prescription" I told him to go out and play tennis for an hour each day, at a suitable time for his studies, for instance, between chapters. I suggested he slow down the pace of his studies and re-insert his favorite sport into his routine. Naturally, he was shocked at the thought of abandoning his books for something that was actually fun, until I redefined the act of playing tennis not as an avoidance of work but a chance instead for the knowledge to seep in and stay.

"Have you ever watered a plant or vegetable garden?" I asked him.

"Of course," he said.

"Well," I continued, "when you see the water start to pool on the top of the soil, do you keep on pouring?"

"No," he replied, "I let it drain in."

"Why?" I asked. "Wouldn't it be quicker to keep on pouring?"

"No," he retorted, "it would just run away over the sides. You have to pour slowly to keep the water in, and stop when it's enough."

"Well, there, you are," I said. "Go play tennis."

He did well on his exams, by the way, and called me to say thanks.

In terms of blue-skying opportunities, racquet sports are among the best. They therefore become a third category for you to consider. They are physical and aerobic, like those in the second category (jogging, exercise bike, etc.) but rather than incorporating a vague visual field, they incorporate a distinctly specific visual stimulus, which involves following a ball around a court. A stringent focus on the ball eliminates all other visual distractions from the field of view. Creative thought is free to roam amidst the eustress of the game. As one squash player once told me, "When you are chasing that little ball around the court, nothing else exists in the world, save for that little ball."

So if you're looking for a more socially acceptable opportunity to blue-sky and let your creative mind run free, one that the working world is more familiar with and therefore more accepting of, consider joining a local lunchtime league for a half-hour game of squash, racquetball, tennis, ping pong, badminton, or even volleyball. Just remember to take a pen and paper, a voice recorder, or your cell phone with you to get those good ideas down when they come. Because they will, if you let them.

I LIKE COFFEE . . .

One of the greatest opportunities for progress through blue-skying can be found within a ritual that has been part of life for over 500 years: taking coffee at a coffee house. Coffee has proven itself over the centuries as a productive tool for cooling down since it provides the ultimate social drink for business.

- It does not impair judgment like alcohol does; in fact, it sharpens the mind through its primary active ingredient, caffeine.
- It is a social drink that can be enjoyed by friends, clients, and business partners.
- It is easily accessible and quite inexpensive.

Coffee is so popular that it is now recognized as the second most traded legal commodity on earth, after oil and petroleum products.[1]

It is said that when coffee first became available in 16th-century Europe, its intellect-sharpening properties were not enthusiastically received by the church, which is not surprising given that the church of those days was an organization whose power was rooted strongly in discouraging creative thought and interpretation among its "client base." Coffee was referred to by some Christians as "the devil's drink." In Rome, a sample of coffee was presented to Pope Vincent III, who had decided to taste it before banishing it. However, as the story goes, upon taking his first sip, he was won over, and he actually baptized it instead.

Coffee, when taken at a coffee house or coffee shop represents another socially acceptable opportunity for blue-skying when it is performed correctly, since it gives the partakers a focal point beyond themselves and their business upon which to reflect for 10 minutes or so. Taking coffee as a blue-skying exercise is best defined by what it is NOT:

- It does NOT happen when you read the paper (or any other reading material) while having coffee. Granted, a coffee break at a coffee shop, which includes reading a newspaper or reviewing your work is still more relaxing than straight-out working at the desk and may provide an opportunity to "hide" undisturbed, but it does not open the door to the higher-level mental creativity of blue-skying. It is just work transferred to another location. *Nice*, yes; *recommended*, yes; but it is not blue-skying.
- It is NOT the coffee you have at your desk. Coffee at your desk is coffee at your desk. A necessary pick-me-up but your desk is not the right location for anything other than the work of the immediate.
- It is NOT the coffee you have in the car, if you are driving.

Instead, coffee-shop blue-skying is about setting the stage for liberating the mind, whether you take your coffee alone, or with others (clients, colleagues, or managers).

For many coffee-shop customers, blue-skying is accelerated through the positive sense of control that comes from placing the order itself. This may sound strange, but it is one of the many reasons for the success of the Starbucks chain. CEO Howard Schultz stated that in creating his coffee-shop empire he wanted to create not just a place to get coffee, but an experience. Interestingly, Mr. Schultz is also on record for saying, "I'm not a big emailer ... it's a crutch that hinders person-to-person communication."[2]

To the uninitiated ear, a large, multi-feature order such as a "grande low-fat, extra-hot, double-foam, half-sweet soy mocha latté" may sound excessive, especially when the same order is echoed back by the employee behind the counter, as if confirming a captain's order on the bridge of a ship. It's a far cry from "coffee, black." But within these minor theatrics, lies a great deal of psychology. The employee—the barista—is first and foremost making sure the order is correct, a fundamental element of establishing customer satisfaction and loyalty. But beyond that, the choice, delivery, and acceptance of such a complex order (how does one measure double foam, exactly?) also helps deliver a dose of esteem to the customer.

Now that may sound silly, psychoanalyzing the transactions of a coffee shop down to elements of self-esteem, but take a moment to place this ritual within the context of the high-speed world outside, where control over time and self-determination are the first things to be wrested away from the average hard-working person. The need for esteem is an essential building-block of self-identity. All humans need to feel it. It is estimated that there are 19,000 possible variations of drinks that can be created from a Starbucks menu, enough to satisfy the specific esteem requirements of each customer, who may not even realize, on a conscious level at least, just how rare it has become to exert such control on a daily basis. By delivering the perfect drink, served at the perfect temperature, in clean, consistent, recognizable surroundings, Starbucks and coffee shops like it help reinforce this sense of esteem, which comforts and satisfies the customer. This makes the customer feel good, of course, which allows the blue-skying process to continue.

A person who sets up her laptop or unpacks her notes at a coffee shop is not fully partaking in the blue-skying process, since her mind is not free to roam—it is looking at notes, But she will still foster great creativity by having stepped away from the ambient momentum of her workplace, replacing it with a neutral noise, the white noise of other people's conversations. This isolates her and gives her a zone of creative space. Access to reliable Wi-Fi systems, of course, makes it easier than ever to focus and to do business away from the office. So all in all it's a productive, *cool* approach to getting work done.

The best approach to blue-skying, however, still has to be when a person just sits still and either watches other people or watched the steam rise from her coffee. This is the antithesis of the high-speed work ethic, of course, but it is where ideas for great new developments are born. It's where problems get solved. Though the temptation is to bring the laptop along, I strongly believe that at least once a week, every busy person should sit down, order a coffee (or tea, or low-sugar soft drink), and just stare into the middle distance.

I LIKE TEA...

Tea, similarly is a refreshment whose benefits go well beyond its actual ingredients and move quite definitively into the beneficial aspects of *slow*. In Japan, the preparing and pouring of tea is considered a high art form, called *chaji*, and great honor is found in being the *teishu*, the house master and tea pourer. The value of *chaji* is not so much in the tea itself, of course. The ceremony gives recognition to the fact that every human encounter is a singular occasion that will never recur. Every aspect of the tea and the ceremony is relished not just for the tea itself, but for what it gives the participants. The classic British cup of tea, similarly, presents most of its value outside of the pot. The biggest selling brand of tea in the UK is PG Tips, a basic, strong blend, made by a subsidiary of Unilever. But it is the ritual that makes British tea what it is: Boiling the water means you have to have a kettle, which means you are somewhere that people can sit down and feel safe, if just for a few minutes.

People pause to enjoy their tea. They slow down just long enough to take in a cup or two. They gather their thoughts, they talk. Tea is used to help people collect themselves after a harrowing experience—not because of any healing properties in the tea itself, necessarily, but those found in the ritual.

All of this may seem like a lot of words to describe coffee and tea breaks, but these two products typify, both literally and figuratively, the value of *slow* in a high-speed world. They also make blue-skying more accessible.

I LIKE CAUSING CREATIVITY

In Chapter 1, we met the wireless PDA owner who was able to get all of his Monday work done on the train, and then pretend it was Tuesday. I mentioned at that point that he would probably have been better off spending his train ride staring out the window, and I meant it.

Previously in this chapter I have attempted to illustrate the value of staring at your shoes during an elevator ride and staring at your coffee in a coffee shop. The idea behind all of these points is this: It takes time for creative thought to step out of the box into which high-speed action has pushed it.

It's hard to say what types of things will come to you when you let your mind relax during blue-skying opportunities. Your ideas might lead to the invention of the next great widget, or they might form the central message of an upcoming presentation. Perhaps they'll be the plans for supper for the next four nights. Your mind knows what it wants to talk about. Whatever that is, it's essential that you first let these ideas come out and then store them somewhere—somewhere, permanent—on paper, for example. And here's the best part and the central point about blue-skying: The more you do it, the more ideas will come.

If you think about the times in your life when you've suffered through a cold or perhaps allergies, you've probably been amazed at the speed and efficiency by which congested sinuses refill with even more disgusting mucus just moments after you have blown your nose. Who would have thought there would be a life lesson in that? Well, there is. Because a creative brain works in much the same fashion, except you use a pen and paper (or a PDA) to receive the results, rather than a Kleenex. The more good ideas you liberate from the short-term memory area of your brain, the more space you make for new creative ideas to take their place, and they will.

The key words here are "liberate" and "from." When ideas are forced to remain where they are, in short-term memory, your creative mind becomes stuffed. It is only when you get them out of there that new ideas can pour forth. Hence the next lesson in the art of blue-skying after actually giving yourself permission to do it, is to keep the ideas coming, simply by receiving them and recording them elsewhere.

Flush them out. And do it regularly. The more you do it, the easier it becomes. And the more opportunity you give to yourself and your future.

Some people might think that encouraging a free flow of ideas in this way is overdoing it. They think that too much creativity, like too much preparation, can stand in the way of actually getting things done. But I disagree, and I disagree as someone who likes to see things get done. I base my argument solidly on the shoulders of all the project managers of the world. Because, in the world of project management, success is best reached through thorough planning. Thorough planning is perfected by discipline. Even when he feels great pressure to get started on the project, the experienced project manager must recognize the greater value in going slowly at this point, rather than rushing ahead. For as he writes out the future life story of the project, on paper or on screen, he envisions it, and his thoughts come out. First, they realistically quantify the elements and actions that go into a project, but then, second, they allow room for other thoughts, for new and better ideas to follow. Though project management might seem to be an analytical process, whereas blue-skying is more synthetic and less consciously purposeful, they have in common this essential principle: Creativity comes from allowing thoughts to appear in the short-term memory area of the mind, at which point they must be flushed out and preserved. Thoughts can't appear in the mind if other thoughts are occupying that space. So, by allowing the thoughts to come forward where they can be captured and recorded, the creative process continues. Slowing down in this fashion works for the practical needs of the time-pressed project manager, just as it can work for everyone.

COMMUTING IN

The commute in to work is a great opportunity for blue-skying. This is why, in Chapter 1, I picked on the guy who owned the wireless PDA. I think there's more value in blue-skying than in working according to Parkinson's Law. On the one hand, the commute presents the same opportunities as the coffee shop and the fountain mentioned earlier in this chapter. The visual vagueness of the passing scenery allows the mind to drift and do its creative thing. This is most obvious for those who commute passively, e.g., by train, bus, or as a car passenger, but it applies also to those who drive. It *is* possible for experienced drivers to both drive and blue-sky at the same time. All it requires is that the driver not use the radio or cell phone.

Blue-skying during the commute not only allows for creative thought to occur, it also contributes greatly to stress management. For most professionals it's a given that negative stress will build up over the day to come. (This, of course, depends on how much they choose to *cool down* during the day.) The more that stress can be alleviated or tempered during the commute in, the better able your mind and body will be to both receive and process additional stressors, and implement *slow* techniques as the day continues. Put another way, those who arrive at the office already stressed, will find their day getting correspondingly worse. Your commute in is a buffer, and should be used as such.

- If you travel by mass transit, even if it is packed full, consider using a CD player or MP3 that plays your favorite kind of music or a spoken-word book as an alternative to doing work or reading. Let the player take you away inside a cone of isolation for the duration of the trip. Yes, you could use that time to work, but my suggestion is that there is greater value (and potential for better work once at the office) by giving yourself this blue-sky oasis at this most stressful of times.
- If you drive, let the traffic be what it will be. No one has ever cleared a traffic jam by shouting at it. If you are running late, call ahead, let them know, and then put your favorite music or a spoken-word book onto your sound system. Though, as a driver, you can't afford to blue-sky as much as a passenger might, you can still cocoon yourself inside your private, acoustically pleasant car interior, which will help you arrive at the office in much better shape.

COMMUTING HOME

The ride home offers similar opportunities for creativity and stress management, the most important of which is the build-up towards healthy sleep. Healthy sleep doesn't just happen overnight. Sleep is an altered state of consciousness brought on by an influx of hormones in the blood. The release of these hormones starts in late afternoon, around 4:00 p.m., and builds up over the next six hours. Tasks that force the body against this natural progression merely end up diluting these sleep chemicals, resulting in a reduced quality of sleep throughout the night. Thus, there is heightened value in actually relaxing and blue-skying on the way home—staring out the window of the train, or enjoying the drive even in clogged traffic by listening to music or spoken-word books. The ride home, in my opinion, is not the place to do more work on the phone, PDA, or laptop. Work is done. It stopped when you left the building. Life happens now, and a successful sleep cycle starts its incubation now.

A lot of people argue with me on this point, and they're welcome to. It's a contentious issue. My conviction seems to go against the mainstream idea that to be "on" all the time is the single pathway to success. But I believe that a comfortable blue-skying commute home is valuable to people through creativity and chemistry. It represents a conscious knowledge of the value of time and effort, which outshines reactionism and pays greater dividends.

KEY POINTS TO TAKE AWAY

- To blue-sky means to stare out at the sky and to let your eyes come to rest while still keeping them open.
- Even when no profound thoughts appear there is still positive action happening below the surface.
- It takes practice for the brain to feel allowed to create in this way.
- One type of blue-skying involves staring at a vague visual field, such as the sky or the ripples of water in a fountain.
- A second type of blue-skying can be achieved through physical preoccupation of the rest of the body, such as jogging, for example, or swimming.
- Racquet sports are a third and very effective blue-skying technique.
- The rituals involved in taking coffee and tea are also excellent blue-skying techniques.
- Creativity comes from freeing your ideas from your short-term working memory. The more you do this, the more ideas will come.
- Project management is a real-world example of how blue-skying can reinforce clarity and creativity for projects of any size.
- Blue-skying on the commute to work offers a far better use of time than doing additional work.
- Blue-skying on the commute home allows for the buildup of healthy sleep chemicals in the bloodstream, which helps ensure top-quality productivity the following day.

HOW TO *COOL DOWN*

Downtime

- When you are in an elevator, do you stare at the walls or reach for your PDA or cell phone?
- Why?
- What would happen if you were NOT to reach for it?
- Are you willing to give it a try?

Blue-Skying (Type 1)

- Do you ever schedule time to sit and blue-sky?
- If yes, what has it done for you?
- If no, why not?

Blue-Skying (Type 2)

- What kinds of aerobic sports do you enjoy?
- How many days a week do you get to enjoy them?
- What do you do with your eyes while exercising (e.g., reading or blue-skying)?

Blue-Skying (Type 3)

- Have you ever played racquet sports?
- How many executives (or people in higher positions than yours) do you know who play?

Coffee

- Have you ever ordered a coffee and enjoyed it without doing work at the same time?

Creativity

- How do you come up with your creative ideas and solutions?
- Which mentors do you have who could share their secrets for creativity?

Commuting and Sleep

- What is your preferred activity during the commute in?
- Why did you choose this?
- What does it do for you?
- What is your preferred activity during the commute home?
- Why did you choose this?
- What does it do for you?
- How well do you sleep at night?
- To what can you attribute your good/bad sleep?

1   Source: International Coffee Organization

2   Murphy, Cait. "Secrets of Greatness: How I Work." *Fortune Magazine*, http://money.cnn.com/2006/03/02/news/newsmakers/howiwork_fortune_032006/index.htm

THE GREATEST PROGRESS
IS GAINED THROUGH REVISITING
THE HUMBLEST ACTIONS.

CHAPTER 6

CREATING A *COOLER* WORKDAY

This chapter looks at some more activities found in a typical workday, to observe just how the act of *cooling down* can contribute to greater productivity. The items here are listed chronologically. Please note, though, that some key elements of the workday (such as meetings and email) have already been covered in previous chapters, and you might therefore wish to refer to those sections.

THE *COOL* ART OF GETTING UP

5:59. One minute left. The numbers on the clock tick over to 6:00 a.m. and the buzzer sounds. You open one eye and look at the clock. No more opportunity left to sink back into blissful slumber. It's time to get up and leave your warm bed behind. In less than an hour you'll be rushing out the door, already late, and another stressful day will be underway.

Sleep is little understood by most people. It's very necessary. If you went without sleep long enough, you'd die. The longest a person has gone without sleep is nine days, and that was in a carefully controlled lab experiment.

But this book chapter is about maximizing your productivity during business hours, long after sleep is done. So why talk about it here? Because when you wake up in the morning, your sleep cycle is not finished. Because sleep, like many other elements of the body, is actually a 24-hour thing. When you exit the sleep phase in the morning, your body is already hard at work doing lots of things on your behalf, and one of them is regulating the chemicals and brainwaves that will ultimately bring you back to sleep.

If your day starts on a stressful note, it will be harder to handle the additional stressors in the hours to come. Not only will this make it more difficult to handle stressors, it ultimately will make it harder to get a good night's sleep later that evening, which will make getting up the next day that much more painful. This, in turn, will reduce your productivity, creating a negative spiral of wasted effort. One major benefit to *cooling down* and taking things slower right from the start is that it maximizes the positive benefits of your entire 24-hour cycle.

The Curse of the Alarm Clock

How do you wake up on a workday? What kind of alarm clock do you have? Odds are it uses a noise to wrest you from sleep. Although some people pride themselves on being able to wake up naturally, and reliably, without an alarm clock, these are the lucky ones. They have discovered a way to stay in sync with their natural sleep cycle. For everyone else, there's the alarm clock.

I believe alarm clocks are fundamentally wrong, and I think also that they are a prime contributor to the counter-productivity of high-speed life. To illustrate my point, let me ask you this: When you are finished with your computer, do you shut it down by pulling the plug or turning off your power bar? No? When you first learned to use a computer, you were probably warned never to just flip the "off" switch, since computers really dislike like being turned off that way. Why? Because computers have to tidy up first. They have to get rid of all kinds of files and temporary memory blocks. If they don't, those blocks will still be there next time the computer is powered up, which degrades its performance and ages it prematurely. That's why the shut-down operation is software-driven, and takes a few seconds or even a minute before the computer is ready to close down. People who use an alarm to wake themselves up are simply flipping the "off" switch on their sleep cycle without tidying up first. This causes a chemical imbalance that can have repercussions for the rest of the day. Sleep is a series of five phases, ranging essentially from light sleep to deep sleep to REM sleep and then back again. We dream for a while and then we don't dream. And then we dream again. People lucky enough to be able to wake up naturally are basically enjoying the results of having finished, tidied up, and put away a complete sleep cycle. By contrast, those who are woken by an alarm are given no chance to close off the cycle, and depending on where you are in it when the buzzer goes, you might wake up feeling fine, or you might end up feeling groggy and tired. Most people experience at least one day per week of feeling groggy, tired, and fighting an ache behind their eyes. Even one day a week like this is too much, since it puts the mental tachometer too far back. There has to be a better way to close down the sleep cycle and build a foundation for a productive day. The waking-up process needs to be slower, *cooler*.

Change Your Alarm Clock

The healthiest type of wake-up device available is one that closes down the sleep process gradually, using subtle increases in light and sound. If your wake-up time is 6:00 a.m., then this clock would come to life at 5:30 a.m. with a gentle low light and very low sound. Over the course of half an hour, these stimuli increase gradually, assisting the body's natural sleep cycle, and helping to bring it to a complete closure.

One of the primary chemicals that brings on and maintains sleep is melatonin, something that is manufactured when there is little or no light. Therefore, the gradual introduction of light, even onto closed eyelids, helps inhibit further production of melatonin, while encouraging the release of stimulant hormones into the bloodstream.

Sound, preferably low-level white noise or quiet music, does the same thing. Together, the light and sound start to stimulate the senses, and awaken the body gradually and in a much healthier fashion.

Use a Timer

For those who do not wish go out and buy a new clock radio, the next recommendation is to use timers. Put a timer on the lamp in your bedroom (not the one on your bedside table, but one further away, if possible), as well as one in your living room and kitchen. Set them to come on at the same time as your alarm. Therefore, even if you must use a harsh alarm to wake up, you will ensure that there is light from the very first moment you open your eyes, which will stimulate hormone production and help to shift your body into wakefulness.

Use Some Sort of Light

If your partner gets to sleep a little while longer than you and prefers that no lights go on in the morning, then use a flashlight. If it is high summer, and it is already light outside, then move to a room where you can open the drapes to let the light in. The objective, in all of these situations, is to use the body's own natural stimulant system to dilute the chemistry of sleep with the minimum of shock.

Lose the Snooze Bar

Another key technique for helping ensure top-quality performance and quicker wakefulness is to no longer use the snooze bar on your alarm clock, since it is not possible to reconnect properly with the full sleep sequence in just nine minutes. It might actually make things worse. Falling back into the primary stages of a new sleep cycle within the time afforded by the snooze bar means that you'll just have to pull yourself out again, and this can hurt more than it helps. Instead, sit up and move your feet around and down, so that you are sitting on the edge of the bed. This reduces the temptation to flop back down. As your eyes start to open and adjust to the light of your timer-activated lamps, start thinking. Think about positive things, about goals, plans, or upcoming leisurely activities. Get the wheels turning, so that together they flush out the chemical remnants of sleep.

Benefit Statement

It sounds harsh, this bright, snoozeless approach to rousing first thing in the morning, but it can truly make a difference between a mediocre day and a top-quality one. By using this technique, you will be:

- More alert first thing in the morning, which will help you to prepare and eat a good breakfast and ensure you leave the house without forgetting anything
- More alert for the whole day
- Able to do more
- Able to remember more
- Able to handle stress better
- Able to digest food better
- More inclined to exercise
- Less prone to fatigue and headaches
- More likely to fall asleep quickly at night
- More likely to enjoy healthier, better sleep
- More able to wake up comfortably the following morning, thus repeating a constructive cycle.

THE BENEFITS OF A *COOL* BREAKFAST

Everyone has heard the old expression that breakfast is the most important meal of the day, yet it still goes under-appreciated and under-used by a great many hard-working people. Some say it's because they have no time. Others say they have no appetite at that hour of the morning. Still others can get by on just a coffee and a muffin or donut.

For those who are lukewarm to the idea of slowing down and having a good breakfast, I would like to suggest that the cost of ignoring breakfast will exact itself throughout the entire day. In Chapter 3, I demonstrated how taking 15 minutes to eat lunch away from your desk will yield far more productivity for the entire day and week to come, and now I must say the same about taking time to eat breakfast—a good breakfast, a real breakfast.

Donuts and muffins always seem so much more appealing than cereal. First, they can be eaten quickly, with little mess, which is perfect for the commuter on the run. Furthermore, the sugar, the colors, the texture, everything about them seems to connect with our senses and satisfies our immediate hunger. They fool our ancient instincts. What the body truly seeks is fruit, grains, and protein—a package of energy for a busy day, but what what we often choose is a low-grade commercial imitation.

The problem with donuts, of course, is that they are made primarily from refined sugars and flour, which deliver a quick burst of energy that lasts for about 20 minutes and works in conjunction with the caffeine boost delivered by coffee and tea to fool the body into thinking it's been fed. Soon after comes the sugar crash as blood sugar imbalances get rebalanced and recompensated by the body's internal mechanisms. Few people who experience a sugar crash actually fall face-first onto their laptop, of course, but if that forehead tachometer mentioned in Chapter 2 were working and visible, the significant drop in processing ability would be noticeable. This is the hidden cost of high-speed food. Muffins may provide a slightly healthier alternative, of course, but most commercially created muffins contain high amounts of fat, including hydrogenated and trans-fats, as well as glucose-fructose and other high-sugar products.

The temporary satisfaction gained from small portable breakfast snacks like these, including the cup-of-coffee-only breakfast, not only negatively impacts mental productivity and energy levels during the morning, they also exert great negative influence on the choices we make for our lunchtime meal.

People who eat small, inefficient breakfasts are much more likely to feel *very* hungry come lunchtime. What's wrong with feeling hungry at lunchtime? Nothing. But there is something wrong with feeling *very* hungry at lunchtime, since extreme hunger leads to more poor food choices. People who are very hungry at lunchtime:

- Seek out fast satisfaction from fast food outlets
- Seek out food with high amounts of starches, fats, and sodium—all great conveyers of taste, but not necessarily of nutrition
- Seek out food based on convenience—fast-moving lines and pre-cooked meals

- Seek out higher proportions of meat and smaller proportions of vegetables.
- Seek out food that doesn't require a lot of chewing
- Eat their food too fast and rely on fast-acting antacids to compensate
- Eat too much, since a great deal can be consumed in 20 minutes.

TIPS for Excellent Breakfast and Morning Snack Choices

- Bran muffin
- Oatmeal
- Zucchini bread
- High-fibre toast
- Yoghurt
- Almonds
- Raisins
- Milk
- Eggs or reduced-cholesterol egg replacements

All of this high-speed reaction to extreme hunger puts extra strain on the body, leading to further reduced ability during the afternoon. The natural lethargy felt by most people at 2:30 p.m. is exacerbated by the blood sugar imbalances caused by fast food, and the sheer effort of its digestion. This reduces the ability to concentrate, which ultimately means work takes longer to get done, with much of it having to be done on the train ride home.

Is there a solution to this? Sure! In the morning, eat foods that take longer to digest—the foods that stick with you longer (see the TIPS box for some suggestions). These will give your body something to keep it occupied and will maintain better internal balance. I'll repeat here just one of the snack suggestions made in Chapter 3, simply because it's the one that many of my past clients and audience members have told me was the most successful of all: the 11:00 a.m. yoghurt. A serving of yoghurt, preferably 0% fat, at 10:45 or 11:00 a.m. helps alleviate growing hunger pains. This allows people to feel less ravenous when lunchtime arrives and therefore allows them to choose more wisely and eat more slowly. It's as simple as that.

The Daily Famine

The other counterproductive result of not having enough time to eat breakfast happens when people skip it entirely. Those who choose this route condemn their body to experiencing "famine mode." When it becomes apparent to your body that food is scarce, because there's none in your stomach by 9:00 a.m., the body reacts by breaking down its own stored energy reserves. It eats from the inside. Now this would be a great concept if your body were to take on those stored fat reserves and whittle them away. But no, stored fat takes weeks to break down. Remember, it's there to help keep hunter-gatherers going through the winter. Instead your starved body goes to work on a different source of easily accessible energy, which is stored inside muscle fiber. This, by the way, is why some unfortunate marathon runners have to undergo that torturous experience 500 yards from the finish line, when they find themselves on hands and knees unable to move any further. During the three hours or so of a race, a marathon runner's body burns up all available stored energy from the muscle tissue. There is nothing left. The poor racer may still have a small amount of body fat around his middle, but three hours is nowhere near enough time to start working on it, and so he collapses. For the high-speed working person who skips breakfast in order to get to the train station on time, similar reflexes operate behind the scenes. Unwilling to undergo famine again, her 50,000-year-old body makes sure that when she finally decides to eat something, a little extra will be stored as fat, just in case another mini-famine happens again tomorrow.

Thus, for the average North American male or female, skipping breakfast or settling for a quick, poor breakfast paves a quick, easy route to weight gain and sluggish mental performance. By contrast, those who *cool down* enough to eat a good breakfast reduce their potential gain of body fat. They fuel their body and mind for a good three or four hours of high-tachometer productivity and accuracy until the next refueling stop just prior to midday.

Finding Time for a Good Breakfast

So where can someone find time for a good breakfast, when mornings are already so busy?

This is an area where we have to counteract the event-to-event mindset, described in Chapter 3. The home-to-work sequence must be redefined, so that if breakfast is currently skipped or rushed, an additional 15 minutes is injected, somewhere between the time we rise and the time we start work. There are two approaches that seem to best fit this mold:

- **The 15-minute at-home breakfast**. What would it take for you to set your rising time just 15 minutes earlier? To give yourself and your family members the chance for a complete breakfast? Or to give yourself a chance at a quiet breakfast before everyone else gets up? Most people react negatively to this statement. Their quick reaction and quick judgment says, "All I can see is losing out on some sleep." But what they tend to forget is that their body would quickly adjust to this new rising time. Almost everyone in the world already demonstrates that changing a sleeping/waking time is possible. They do it twice a year, when they switch from Daylight Savings Time to Standard Time and back again. And that's a whole hour! Within three days the body readjusts. It can be done. Getting up 15 minutes earlier can be easily achieved, and with just a little practice, the new rising time will be hardly noticeable.

- **The 15-minute breakfast before work**. If it is not possible to get up 15 minutes earlier for whatever reason, the next best approach is to invest in these minutes elsewhere—somewhere that is neither work nor home. Perhaps a favorite coffee shop, food court, park bench, or the privacy of your car (once parked). Not everyone has the budget or the desire to pay money every day for food from a restaurant or coffee shop, but that's no problem. There are many types of portable foods that can be brought from home and will not perish if eaten within an hour of leaving the refrigerator. Bananas, yoghurt, home-made muffins, bagels, a thermos of coffee, tinned fruit, even a sealable dish of healthy breakfast cereal along with a second, sealable thermos cup of cold milk are all available and reliable. This breakfast between home and work requires an adjustment to the "event-to-event" mindset that has us all racing from home to work in once single action, but once again, its payoffs are great. The importance of choosing to have your 15-minute breakfast before you get to work, rather than *at work* is probably obvious. Once at work, your mind and body will be in *work mode*, prone to interruptions, requests, distractions, and work itself, a situation in which the idea of eating properly quickly gets pushed aside.

The bottom line here is that productivity starts with fuel, and fuel must be delivered properly at the start of the day. This requires a small amount of time, a small amount of *slow*.

THE COMMUTE IN

The daily commute is that twin set of episodes in the day in which time is spent battling the elements in an attempt to get to work reasonably punctually. For people in a home office, this might simply mean a short trip up or downstairs. For others, it might mean getting to different locations to visit different customers each day, and for the majority, it means getting to your place of employment to carry on with the projects and challenges at hand.

Not wishing to repeat myself, I would like to state simply that the difference between a *cool*, calm commute in, and a frenzied stress-filled one will be visible in all of your actions and abilities for the day to come. That is why in Chapter 3, "The *Cool* Approach to Commuting," I highlighted the value of a slower drive, and in Chapter 5, I advocated the use of this time for blue-skying rather than taking on additional work as per the demands of Parkinson's Law.

The Daily Warm-Up

What I wish to add to this is the value of the changed mindset that a *cooled-down* commute can provide. The commute is a mental changing room. It is where people must shift from home mode to work mode and then back again at the end of the day. It's an opportunity to ramp up to that level of focus and preparedness that will ensure top-quality productivity and stress management throughout the entire day. Recall in Chapter 2 the analogy of the NBA player and the need for warm-up, both for him and, by extension, for your colleagues around a meeting room table. So, too, it is necessary to do this on the commute in, so that there is greater opportunity for you to handle appropriately the immediate requests that will be waiting when you arrive at your workplace. We must eliminate the "event-to-event" mindset that defines the commute as a mere inconvenience and use it instead as an opportunity.

A Mentoring Opportunity: Carpooling

The work-bound and home-bound commutes both offer yet another opportunity for personal growth and profit by mentoring with carpool colleagues. In Chapter 9, I will challenge you about your mentoring commitments, both in seeking out a mentor and in being one. The benefit, as I describe more fully in that chapter, has to do with not only hearing another person speak, but in also hearing yourself, as you will always be your own best audience and critic when it comes to creative thought. The secret, however, is to let those thoughts escape your short-term memory for a moment by speaking them out loud and have them reinforced by hearing them spoken. One of the best ways you can do this is by changing how you view your commute. Turn it from a solitary race against time to a learning opportunity, by sharing the drive—carpooling.

How to Enjoy a Smoother Start to Your Commute

Create an evening checklist that reminds you to:

- Listen to the latest weather report. Will there be frost or snow tomorrow? If so, plan for the time required to clear the driveway and car of snow and ice. Will there be rain tomorrow? If so, allow extra time for the commute.
- Consider purchasing a windscreen cover that actually prevents frost from forming.

- Make sure all items needed are accounted for, e.g., files, keys.
- Make sure your cell phone is charged, or charge it up overnight.
- Make a realistic assessment of how long it actually takes you to get from your front hall to your office. Not an optimistic one, but one that factors in traffic, weather, and other realities. Then add 15% more. Create a departure schedule that favors a "pessimistic" estimate, and you will find the trip less stressful.
- When confronted with arrogant drivers or pushy commuters, choose sympathy over anger. Rather than meet their anger with your own, view them as people who are suffering. Feel pity for them, silently. It's a remarkably calming technique.

Throughout this book I highlight many situations in which the value of face-to-face communications outweighs the perceived advantages of high-speed activity. Talking together within a carpool is a great central example of this difference. Someone might ask, for example, what the difference would be between conversing with people who are physically in the car (or on the train) with you, versus talking on a cell phone. The answer is significant: When a person is talking to you on a cell phone, she cannot make eye contact, and she cannot read your facial and non-verbal messages, and she doesn't know about the specific driving challenges you are currently facing. She continues to talk, and the expectation from both parties is that the conversation must continue at this pace, even if traffic is becoming challenging. This is why, as I mention in Chapter 2, talking on a cell phone while driving causes significant impairment: The driver's faculties are largely taken over by the conversation due to his inability to meter it in any other way. By contrast, a discussion in a car takes advantage of numerous interpersonal dynamics, in which the conversation can be attended and paced through body language, and even paused if the driver needs his full concentration and reaction abilities. Mentoring and being mentored in a carpool is part networking, part blue-skying, and part education. It makes even the most congested route more of a pleasure and far less of a waste of time.

The Daily Warm-Up for the Home-Based Professional

A similar warm-up happens for those whose office is at home. It is always highly recommended that a home-based professional assign a room, or at least a corner of a room as a designated workspace. This is not merely for organization's sake; it serves to create a mental division between work life and home life, just as a commute does for others. People with home offices tend to subscribe to Parkinson's Law just as much as anyone else, even if they don't own a wireless PDA. The temptation to check and answer email at 10:30 at night is just as strong. However, those who create a designated space, and who take the time to commute to and from it, rather than bringing work to the dining room table, allow a mental transition to take place. This makes it easier to let go of work in the evening and to turn away from it when the day is done, even if it's only six steps from the kitchen to the office.

A *cool* commute, for all working people, is an opportunity to don the "work suit" in time for the arrival at the workplace, and more importantly, to take it off again when it's time to go home.

PLANNING AND ASSESSING THE VALUE OF TASKS

Once we get to work, of course, we then have to get to work. Management guru Peter Drucker said it many years ago: "There is nothing so useless as doing efficiently that which should not be done at all." This prompts the question: Are the tasks that you plan to do, or more precisely the tasks that you actually do, important enough to be done, by you, now? How can you tell? What is your benchmark? What do the tasks mean with regard to your working goals for the day? For the week? For the year? What will they mean this time next year? What does your manager think about the tasks you choose to do? Are business and speed causing you to react rather than pro-act? How can you tell? Is high-speed technology just allowing you to do unimportant things faster? What can you do to replace busy-ness with business?

That's a barrage of questions, but they lead back to the central statement once again that high-speed reactionism costs more than it makes. Planning and assessment require that you slow down before moving ahead, long enough to ensure that your efforts are being wisely used. Many people turn to their email first thing in the morning. For some, as we've seen, this may be essential to their primary line of work. But for others, it's merely reaction without strategy. Are you able to take some time, seconds, even, to think through your actions before acting? Such an action often yields some surprising and helpful revelations. Consider the following case study:

Case Study: Working for a Workaholic

Sally was a hard-working professional who came to me seeking help on what she thought was a problem with procrastination. "I tend to put things off until the end of the day," she said, and this was causing her obvious distress. Together we reviewed her workload and her work style. What we discovered was that she was really quite an organized person. However, her manager was a workaholic who never seemed to leave the office before 9:00 p.m. To match this, Sally, who was eager to appear as a team player and a responsible professional, had also been staying longer and longer so that she could complete her work and deliver it to her manager. What appeared to be procrastination was really Sally's unconscious desire to reorganize her workload so that the important things were still there to be done around the close of the day. In this way she was "forced," by her own will, to stay later in order to hand them in and appear indispensable. Sally had no time to assess the circumstances that caused this to happen, namely the personality of her manager. She had been just plowing ahead, unaware of the dark path down which such high-speed pursuits were leading her. What would you advise Sally if she had come to you for advice?

My recommendation was threefold: First, I recommended that she take some time to understand her manager's personality and approach to work. This included talking to a mentor on the nature of workaholism and how to deal with it. The time required to do this, however, would pay off in her improved ability to approach and negotiate with her manager. Second, I recommended that, armed with her new knowledge, she and her manager should step away from the grindstone and discuss their different schedules with an aim to negotiating a revised and mutually satisfactory schedule of tasks and expectations. Third, I recommended Sally review the questions in the opening paragraph of this section (Are the tasks that you plan to do, or more precisely, the tasks that you actually do, important enough to be done, by you, now? How can you tell?), prior to embarking on, or saying yes to additional requests or scheduling tasks for earlier or later times in the afternoon.

The expression used in project management circles is that those who fail to plan, plan to fail. In Sally's case, as with so many other time-pressed, high-speed people, this applies equally well. Taking the time to plan and work things out allows you to better know what you're getting into. Otherwise, momentum will just carry you along on its blind path, at your expense.

Planning for Meetings

We had a good look at meetings in Chapter 2, and offered a few tips on running them better. But what about your reaction to a meeting invite? This is another example where a *cool* approach can help win back a significant portion of your day for your own use. Whether the invitation comes by way of voicemail message, a direct face-to-face request, or worse, the meeting is simply inserted into your calendar by way of an electronic scheduling system, those who are able to assess its worth and then negotiate accordingly stand to gain more time to do more of their other tasks than those who willingly comply. When you are asked to attend a meeting, is it possible to slow down and ask some or more of the following questions?

- Will you need me for the entire meeting?
- For how long will you need me?
- Can I negotiate a late arrival or early departure while you're covering items that don't concern me?
- Will you be sending the agenda in advance so that we can prepare for the meeting?

Such questions are never intended to challenge the authority of the requestor. They're intended to step away from candid reactionism and to seek alternatives to simple "death-in-harness." Just because meetings have been run a certain way for many years does not mean we no longer have the opportunity to offer suitable alternatives. All such discussions must be approached with respect, of course, especially towards the chairperson. However, much can be said for speaking in the language of mutual benefit.

- You can communicate to the chairperson how your partial attendance will allow you to give your undivided attention to the meeting, for the parts that concern you.
- You can demonstrate how your departure will help refocus the group more tightly for the next agenda item.
- You can demonstrate the value of the work that you will be able to do prior to and upon leaving the meeting early.

Negotiation, in this scenario, as with all others, must always aim for the win-win. This is a language that all people understand, and when phrased correctly, they will be able to visualize how the results will benefit them.

Alleviating Confusion While Prioritizing or Multitasking

One final demonstration of the power of *cooling down* comes from the alleviation of confusion and stress when trying to prioritize multiple conflicting activities. This is a situation in which overload happens quickly, and the cost is great. In Chapter 5, in the section entitled, "I like Causing Creativity," I used the unusual metaphor of clogged sinuses to illustrate the way the human brain processes creative thought. Most important, I pointed out the value of recording your ideas, and in so doing, more creative ideas will rush in to fill the space. Later, in Chapter 8, I will describe how taking time to write things out actually helps us to cope with or even alleviate fears, simply through the act of making them "solid," that is to say, getting them on paper. This technique has great value for anyone who is struggling with the mental overload of handling more than one task or urgency at a time: Slow down and separate the items on paper.

- Dealing with multiple static tasks: Let's say you have a number of tasks, big and small, to take care of within the same two-hour timeframe. You could choose to grab the first one and run with it, or you could take a moment to write out the urgency and timelines of each, and then take this plan to the stakeholders in order to involve them in the negotiation and resolution of the conflict. Although it is not easy to go back to one or more managers and ask them to help you in reprioritizing these tasks, I suggest it be done for the following reason. Liberating your mind from the pressure and confusion that swirls about inside short-term memory during these scenarios will liberate a greater amount of creative energy and focus, since the brain no longer has to "hold these things in its hands." If you want a fast path to clear thought, then writing down and assessing conflicting problems, especially in conjunction with the stakeholders, will get you further, faster.

- A similar principle applies with dynamic tasks, such as phone calls, drop-in visitors, and other incoming messages. No-one can handle more than one at a time. Even people who are attracted to high-speed, high-pressure work know there are (or should be) rules in place to ensure nothing gets forgotten. Just ask a day trader. Or an E.R. nurse. Or a journalist. When people come knocking at your door asking for an immediate response, give them the signal that says, "Wait until I can get this thought down on paper (or saved as a file) before I change my train of thought." This is the crucial act of closure that wraps up every activity. Before you attend to the next incoming email, or the next person hovering over your desk, slow down, complete the task at hand, take a breath, and then move on.

GETTING ENOUGH EXERCISE

Whatever day it happens to be that you are reading these words, 1,000 Canadian baby boomers (those born between 1946 and 1964), as well as 7,918 American baby boomers will turn 60 today. Happy birthday! For them, and for those who follow them, the threat of heart disease is ever present. In the opinion of many cardiologists, dieticians, and other professionals, this is due, in part, to a *laissez-faire* attitude towards personal health, combined with the requirements of a busy career and consequently letting exercise slide. As a result, cardiovascular disease (CVD), which includes high blood pressure, coronary heart disease, and stroke is now the single leading cause of death in both Canada and the United States.[1]

Case Study: "I have no time for exercise."

Shauna worked for the media department of a large organization. She used to enjoy going to the gym. She saw and felt the benefits of regular workouts—better sleep, better mood, better resistance to colds, overall better feeling. But as the pressures of work became greater, her workouts were always the first thing to be sacrificed. First, occasionally, and then more regularly, she rescheduled them until finally her running shoes started to gather dust.

She said, "Every day the work takes me to 5:30 or 6:00, sometimes later. It doesn't make sense to go to the gym at 6:30. If I did, that would mean I'd not get home until 8:30 or later."

Shauna was focused on her work, on being busy. But she was not able to perceive that being busy and being productive are not the same things. As we have seen, email, meetings, and distractions make people feel busy, and indeed they may be legitimate components of work. But she was not able to see how speed and overload had blinded her to being able to tell the difference.

Great Ways to Reassign Work

- Observe patterns in your day and week to see where quieter times exist.
- Schedule your most important tasks for early morning and defend the time against intrusion.
- Set up a buddy system with a colleague, who can cover for you and vice versa.

- Identify tasks that can and should be delegated. How many tasks are you currently doing that could be done by someone else?
- Negotiate. There's most always room for a suitable alternative to now.

When Shauna did an audit of her work patterns, including the most important types of work, the nature and frequency of the emails she was responding to, and the "human element" (the expectations of her boss and of her external and internal clients), she realized that the key work components could be reassigned to specific hours. She applied more conscious control over casual conversations and drop-in visitors, and made a point to not let time slip by. Her careful choice of meals and snacks kept her alertness level high, and most important, she took time to ask her manager outright whether a change to her schedule was possible. She and her manager worked on this together and agreed that she could leave work a half-hour earlier, provided that her key assignments were up to date. She agreed to come in a half-hour earlier on her workout days and most importantly, she made sure to reserve time with her manager once a week, every week, to demonstrate how her productivity had actually improved through this new pattern.

Shauna found she was also better able to deal with her colleagues, some of whom observed her early departure and immediately questioned her loyalty and team spirit. Shauna found she was able to educate her team through communication. She explained to them how the work they needed from her would still be completed on time, that she herself remained available and accountable throughout the day, and she showed them how her open-door policy was not going to be adversely affected. With their needs and concerns met, Shauna was able to condition herself and her colleagues into working well within these slightly modified timelines. Her slightly earlier departure allowed her three workouts a week, and she was still able to get home in time for dinner.

The success factor was not Shauna's dedication to working out; it was that she took the time to slow down and communicate with her manager and with her co-workers. That's what gave her the permission and the freedom to go to the gym.

When Is a Good Time to Exercise?

People often ask me what the best time of day is for exercise. Such a question can be answered, but not simply. There are many factors to take into account, since not all exercise is equal. Running outdoors is much more difficult than running on a treadmill, due to sidewalk friction, air resistance, and changes in surface angle and grade. Lifting weights for three sets of 20 reps has a different impact on muscle development than six sets of 10 reps. Doing cardiovascular exercise with a mid-level active heart rate for 30 minutes has profoundly different effects on the body than does high-speed sprinting for 20 minutes.

As people age, their bodies react differently to food (including excess food), sleep, stress, excess, deprivation, and exercise. That's why it's so important to know yourself; to slow down long enough to hear your body tell you what it wants and when. Are you morning oriented? If so, are you able to get in a workout before work? Some people find it easy to get up at 5:00 a.m. and hit the gym. It's an excellent way to start a day. Others, however, cannot do that. Many people cannot face exercise first thing in the morning, no matter how good it might be for them. So, then, what remains for morning-oriented people, whose best time for energy and activity is the morning, but who can't get to the gym before work and who also can't delay work to spend time at the gym? Does that mean they're doomed to not get any exercise at all? That need not be the case.

Some people may be able to put into effect the same type of flexibility that Shauna demonstrated in the case above, but in reverse. They might renegotiate start times so they can arrive at the office a little later, and, if need be, work a little later to balance it out. Others might be able to find the time within the workday. More and more employers are providing on-site fitness centers or corporate health club memberships along with the permission to use them. Refer, once again to the AstraZeneca example in Chapter 4.

Still others may be able to adopt Shauna's situation more directly by setting up staggered departure times, and by communicating the value and benefits of doing so to their manager and team. When the only time available for exercise is late afternoon, even if late afternoon is not your optimum time, it is still possible to make best use of the opportunity by slowing down and choosing a food intake schedule for the day more carefully.

In the *Fortune* magazine article "How I Work," the CIO of Pimco puts it as follows:

> For a portfolio manager, eliminating the noise is critical. You have to cut the information flow to a minimum level. You could spend your whole day reading different opinions. For me, that means I don't answer or look at any emails I don't want to. Other than for my wife, I'll only pick up the phone three or four times a day. I don't have a cell phone, I don't have a [wireless PDA]. My motto is, I don't want to be connected—I want to be disconnected.
>
> The most important part of my day isn't on the trading floor. Every day at 8:30 a.m., I get up from my desk and walk to a health club across the street. I do yoga and work out for probably an hour and a half, between 8:30 and 10:00. There have only been two or three times in the past 30 years when someone has come across the street and told me I should get back to the office. One of them was the 1987 market crash.
>
> There's an understanding here that that's my haven. Some of my best ideas literally come from standing on my head doing yoga. I'm away from the office, away from the noise, away from the Bloomberg screens—not to mention that standing on your head increases the blood flow to your brain.
>
> After about 45 minutes of riding the exercise bike and maybe ten or 15 minutes of yoga, all of a sudden some significant light bulbs seem to turn on. I look at that hour and a half as the most valuable time of the day.[2]

The Benefits of Slow Exercise

All exercise, when done correctly, is good. But the benefits of *cooling down* reveal themselves in the exercise room just as they do in other areas. For people who are looking to burn off that spare tire of stored fat during the workweek, slow exercise is far more efficient than a high-impact workout. Fast aerobics may be good for getting the cardiovascular system in shape, but they don't burn stored energy as efficiently. Fat burning happens when exercise is of lower impact but longer duration, for instance, 20 to 30 minutes on a cycling machine or treadmill, three times a week.

Maintaining Commitment

Most people who exercise regularly notice by the second week that the exercise itself becomes addictive. The body gets used to exercise, and starts to "ask" for it. However for the first few days, getting into a habit may seem difficult. One of the best approaches is to buddy up—to make a commitment with a friend to visit the gym together. This makes procrastination or rescheduling more difficult since it would inconvenience two people, not just one.

Also, consider entering your workouts into your calendar as recurring activities. This *reifies* the event, making it real both in your own mind as well as in the minds of other people in your working world.

Use a log to keep track of your workouts, laps, minutes, etc. A log is useful in four distinct ways:

- First it serves as a guide and a goal: you have a target to aim for.
- Second, it is a written commitment. As we have already seen, written material carries far greater weight and credibility than do thoughts that circulate in short-term memory.
- Third, the act of checking something off as completed is a powerful reinforcer. It feels good to put a check mark next to today's scheduled exercise, and to say, "Yes, I've done that."
- Fourth, it is less pleasurable to skip a workout when it's written, planned, and scheduled. It is crucial, especially during the first two weeks of a new exercise regime, not to miss any workouts.

Averting Boredom

Do you find long workouts boring? Is that one of the reasons why it is so difficult to motivate yourself to do it daily? It's true. Thirty minutes on an exercise bike can seem extremely dull to anyone who has just stepped out of their high-speed working world. But there are solutions. Here are a few:

- **Music.** Your favorite tunes are more accessible and portable than ever before. It is easy to put together a collection of high-energy dance tunes by your favorite artists as a custom soundtrack to your workouts. Download them from a tunes site and play them on CD, MP3, or any other format. Studies have shown that workouts are more effective when there is danceable music present since the beat keeps the body in pace and passes the time pleasantly.

- **Spoken-word books.** These, too, are available in both downloadable format and also by mail. (Recommended suppliers are listed in this chapter's How to Cool Down section. There are thousands of book titles that have been recorded, often by well-known actors. Each CD is generally an hour long, perfectly timed for a great workout. View exercise as an opportunity to get in shape and catch up on all those books you've been meaning to read. But don't read them; listen to them!

- **Movies.** These are also available in "rental-by-mail" formats, just like spoken-word books. With portable DVD players costing under $100 in some cases, it's easy to prop one up on the console of a treadmill or exercise cycle and let the time slide by.

- **Thinking with your eyes closed.** Though this one may not seem as stimulating as the previous suggestions, exercising on a safe setup, such as a treadmill, exercise bike, or stair climber means you can do it with your eyes closed. This allows your blue-skying thoughts to arrive in good form. They're yours for the taking, every day, and it gets easier with practice. Once you know that you will have 30 minutes of daily eyes-closed aerobic exercise, creative thoughts, positive thoughts, deep thoughts willingly appear before you. I recommend this technique heartily, but with two reminders:

1) Make sure your setup is safe, e.g., no loose shoelaces or other potential dangers and 2) Make sure to have something close by to record your great ideas—they're too valuable to lose.

Building Muscle the Slow Way

For people who are looking to build more muscle or develop muscle tone, it may surprise you to learn that lifting weights slowly is far better than doing "power sets" or using the "clean and jerk" approach. Lifting weights more slowly enables you to employ proper technique, which ensures the right muscle groups are being used and challenged. The human body is capable of using numerous other muscle groups to compensate or share the load. This means that many people who invest the time to work out with weights waste a great deal of it through improper technique. (The actual technique and motion required is best learned by taking the time to ask a qualified trainer at your health club to work with you.) Proper, *cool* technique also reduces the risk of injury, since the weight is moved in the proper direction, offering the right type of resistance to the muscle. In addition to using the wrong muscle groups and/or risking injury, people who work their weights or weight machines too quickly tend to use momentum, not strength to move the weight. This is a subtle, unintentional form of cheating that reduces the demand on the muscles being trained as soon as the weight gets moving. A good weight movement should be slow and steady on the way out and on the way home, using care and focus to keep it safely in line. This, of course, reflects the *slow* principle perfectly: the difference between doing something of substance versus the false satisfaction of just feeling busy. True productivity, both at the desk and in the gym, really does require a *cool* approach.

---

8 Ways That *Cooling Down* Can Improve Your Company Right Now

- **Development of Communities of Practice**. Improvement comes from education, but not all education is classroom-based. Communities of practice are groups of people who have in common a particular interest or procedure within the company's operations. They are informal, as opposed to a formally structured team, and tend to meet, either in person or on-line, at regular intervals to share knowledge about their area of expertise. Allowing time for employees to participate in Communities of Practice helps to both distribute and generate knowledge and expertise.

- **Establishment of Organizational Memory**. One of the greatest losses a company can face is when its knowledge base walks out the door due to downsizing, attrition, or retirement. The concept of Organizational Memory recognizes that the collective knowledge and wisdom of a workforce must be transferred and retained if the company itself is to have a future. This requires time for employees and managers to step away from immediacies and instead establish traditions and opportunities to systematically transfer this knowledge through mentors, classrooms, experiential scenarios, and interviews.
- **Identification and Treatment of Burnout and Stress**. Not everyone who calls in sick on a Friday is faking it. Similarly, not everyone who is at work today should be there. Can you tell the difference? People who are burning out will soon be lost to the company. Through absenteeism, presenteeism, resignations, and long-term illnesses these assets quickly lose their potential for the company's bottom line, and worse may lead to personal tragedy. Managers and organizations who allow time to step out of the silo and observe what is truly going on in the heads and hearts and eyes of their staff stand to keep them around, healthy, loyal, and productive.
- **Elimination of Firefighting and its Cascade Effect**. Firefighting has a quadruple cost: first, the time and stress involved in fighting the fire; second the need to reschedule and revisit the tasks that were put aside in order to fight the fire; third, the ongoing concern among employees of the fire breaking out again; and fourth, the perception in the minds of the customer, who must balance your quick action in fighting a fire against the existence of the fire in the first place. Though fires and crises inevitably happen, it is the company who sits

its people down and works in post-mortem review—to identify how to mitigate such fires in the future that stands to refocus its employees' energies on higher value tasks.

- **Pattern Identification: There are busy times in the year and quieter times.** There are times when people take vacation, there are long weekends, and then there's the Christmas/ holiday season. Patterns can easily be recognized by people who take the time to lay them out on a tangible surface, such as a wall calendar. Pattern identification can help offset personnel shortages, firefighting, deadline crunches, and can also be instrumental in influencing the needs and expectations of the customer.

- **Parallel and Bottom-Up Learning.** Whether implementing large-scale change or simply seeking smaller-scale continuous improvement, more can be done through parallel learning scenarios, in which all levels of an organization together follow a systematic model of inquiry, innovation, and testing. This requires more time than traditional top-down initiatives, but pay off in heightened motivation, buy-in, and, of course, improvement.

- **Conflict Management.** Conflicts often escalate because people confuse the issue with the individuals involved. The best time to resolve a conflict is before it becomes a conflict, when it is still just an irksome issue between two people. This requires time to slow down and observe. Sources of conflict don't always go away by themselves, but time spent in advance usually wins back much more later on.

- **Superordinate Goals and Motivation.** Companies that take time to demonstrate to its employees the large-scale vision of a single project, or of the company in general, will yield greater productivity, since emotion-based humans work primarily on emotion. Goals are more than a framed mission statement on the wall, though. Managers need to connect, human to human if they are to effectively communicate superordinate goals as well as hear unfettered feedback.

KEY POINTS TO TAKE AWAY

- Sleep should be observed as a series of cycles. Waking up is the closing down of this series, and should be approached gradually, rather than with shock.
- Light reduces the sleep hormone melatonin and stimulates the body to activity. Use light in any form you can as soon as you wake up.
- Our physical body structure hasn't changed in 50,000 years. Excess energy is stored as fat.
- Highly processed fast foods answer the call for nutrition but don't deliver in the same way.
- Sugar swings yield great influence on lunchtime meal choices, which leads to reduced ability during the afternoon.
- Eating more of the right things slower will maintain better internal balance.
- Those who skip breakfast entirely condemn their body to experiencing "famine mode," which actually contributes to weight gain.
- A fast-food breakfast or skipping breakfast entirely not only depletes mental and physical energy but also leads to poor food choices at lunchtime, which can adversely affect afternoon productivity.
- Allow time for a 15-minute breakfast either at home or somewhere else other than the workplace.
- The commute to work serves as a daily warm-up that gets the mind in the right place for work. The commute home does the same in reverse.
- Carpooling is a great opportunity for mentoring.
- Tasks should be assessed and valued before moving ahead with them in order to avoid the blindness that can come from reactionism.
- Multitasking and prioritization are best served by slowing down, writing down, and then negotiating.
- The best time to exercise depends on your job, your metabolism, and your ability to communicate with your manager.
- Slow exercise is far more efficient than a high-impact workout for burning fat.
- Slow weight-training reps are far better for building muscle than fast ones.

HOW TO *COOL DOWN*

Getting Up and Waking

- How do you get up in the morning?
- What sort of alarm clock do you use? Is it shrill or gentle? Immediate or gradual?
- What time do you get up in relation to the time you need to properly prepare for the day?
- Would you be able to get up 15 minutes earlier?
- Have a look at different (and better) types of alarm clocks that will help the waking process through the introduction of light. Remember, sleep is governed in large measure by a hormone called melatonin, which the body can only manufacture in the absence of light. To counteract the sleep-inducing effects of melatonin, you have to have light available. This is why these clocks work so well; they introduce light gently, while you are still asleep, and start the stimulation up to half an hour prior to your desired waking time. Samples are available at the *Cool Down* section of my website at www.bristall.com.
- Use timers. Use a timer to turn on a light, perhaps in the living room or kitchen, so that the light is on by the time you move from the bedroom to the kitchen. This will give your body an additional light stimulation.
- If you drink coffee in the morning, use a coffee machine with a timer, so that the aroma of coffee meets you on first waking. This is an additional source of sensory input that will allow you to break away from the sleep pattern. It's also nice to have the coffee ready.

Exercise

- When is your best time for exercise?
- What is your favorite type of exercise?
- How easy/difficult is it to implement regular exercise into your workday?

- What arguments or negotiations could you present to your manager or colleagues?
- Who could you buddy up with to ensure your exercise regularly?

Recommended Suppliers

- Music is available through numerous online services, including iTunes.
- If you work out at home, Pandora (www.pandora.com) is an online radio station in which you program your own music. Tunes that share similar properties are offered to expand your collection of favorites, and over time, the system learns your tastes to a very accurate degree. You can listen through your PC.
- Spoken word books are available by mail through SimplyAudio-Books (www.simplyaudiobooks.com). Your local library is another resource.
- Movies are available by mail through NetFlix (www.netflix.com) and BlockBusterOnline.

---

1   Data for this paragraph taken from The U.S. Census Bureau, The American Heart Association, and The Canadian Heart and Stroke Association.

2   Murphy, Cait. "Secrets of Greatness: How I Work." *Fortune Magazine*, http://money.cnn.com/2006/03/02/news/newsmakers/howiwork_ fortune_032006/index.htm

IN ALL TRANSACTIONS

THE CUSTOMER'S TRUE PURCHASE

IS YOU. NOTHING ELSE.

CHAPTER 7

BECOMING A COOLER PERSON

THE POWER OF KNOWING

Are you noticeably great or are you one of the crowd? How would other people answer that question about you? What does your image say to those around you? Is it helping you get ahead? Is speed revealing ragged edges and imperfections? Most importantly, how do you know?

Human beings, including all of your colleagues and clients, take in 70 percent of what they know and understand about the world around them by way of visual cues and non-verbal communication. In Chapter 2, case studies of Bruno and Karen, and later, of the locomotive engineers highlighted the effects of a diminished ability and opportunity to read body language in negotiation situations. They quickly caused intellectual isolation. People really do judge situations and other people by what they see and take in. Consequently, it is of great strategic value for those who wish to impress, influence, and get further ahead, that they slow down and learn more about how they come across in all manner of situations. This is what this chapter is about. It looks at some of the key areas in which progress can be gained through a combination of conscious awareness and preparation.

Knowing What You Look Like

This section is not a chapter on choosing wardrobes and hairstyles. There are many other books that do that. For our purposes, it's not just *what* you look like that counts; it's that you *know* what you look like that is truly important. Your chosen style of dress and presentation will penetrate the mind of the observer and will travel first by way of his emotional routing system, which means that judgments, positive or negative, and feelings of attraction, indifference, or repulsion are made on the spot. This is very powerful stuff.

The people who *know* this, and who are in control of their image, have a creative intellectual advantage over those who do not. Here's how they do it:

- *Eye contact.* Primarily, impressions are made through eye contact—the windows of the soul. Not only is eye contact with others stronger and more frequent when you are aware of your visual presentation, the "shape" of the eye, that is to say the highly expressive areas of skin and facial muscles that surround the eye present a more focused, more direct appearance. To use two extreme examples, think of Mick Jagger and Woody Allen. Mick Jagger, one of the most charismatic and successful entertainers in music history, has a uniquely piercing visual approach; he maintains eye contact far longer than most people, and the skin and muscles that form his eyelids and upper face appear to "hone in" on the person to whom he's speaking in an unmistakable fashion. Compare this to the characters played by comedian Woody Allen—characters renowned for their neuroticism and lack of confidence. Although these are merely fictional people, Woody Allen capitalizes on his own facial characteristics—raised eyebrows, wide-open eyes, and a generally sad and preoccupied demeanor to convey a person more confused than focused.

Obviously, the goal for any person wishing to advance in life is to aim for the camp in which facial signals direct their energy outwards, towards other people, rather than inward upon a worried self. The more aware you are of how you look, the easier it is for your facial muscles to do this, and therefore project your charisma silently but effectively.

Tips for Managing Your Image

- Schedule your travels to always arrive early. Make sure you can get to a location with a mirror so you can ensure you look the way you want. Remember, this is not an exercise in vanity; it's an exercise in personal control.
- Carry a travel kit that contains all the toiletries and tools required to keep looking consistently good. (This applies to men as well as women.) This can include:
  - Headache relief medication (Aspirin, Tylenol, etc.)
  - A pocket mirror and hairbrush
  - Breath spray/mints
  - Spot remover for clothing
  - Crease relaxant spray for clothing
  - A cloth to buff up shoes
  - A lint brush
  - Scissors for trimming stray threads
  - A tiny tube of superglue for sticking buttons back on—quicker than sewing
  - A snack (such as a granola bar or dried fruit bar).
- Hire the services of an image consultant to gain a professional outside opinion on clothing, hair, jewelry, and other visuals. Use this person's extensive knowledge of others to help build and maintain a consistently impressive look.
- Choose the clothes you plan to wear for the days ahead and organize them in a sequence that will remove the need for decision-making in early mornings.
- Practice knowing how you look by videotaping yourself. This is the only way to really know, since it shows you in "real image," as opposed to "mirror image" as mirrors do. Schedule a conversation with a friend or family member expressly for the purposes of videotaping yourself. Hold a conversation as you would with a client, manager, or colleague, and review your mannerisms, eye contact, the frequency of smiles, posture, and body language and the way your clothes, glasses, hair, etc., appear. This is a very revealing exercise, but that's what it's for.

- *Body language and posture.* This awareness further translates into effective body language and posture. People who know what they look like walk into a situation fully in control. Their knowledge about their appearance relaxes their mind and liberates their creativity. It allows for their conversations to be well-guided, relaxed and time-efficient. It allows them to recall and relate key facts and discussion points and maintain active, interesting discussions. It allows them to listen actively to others and project sincerity and interest. These are the types of qualities that impress people.

Knowing What You Sound Like

Once you have a handle on what you look like, it's also worth a moment to find out what you sound like. It's hard to accurately tell, given that when you hear your own voice, it gets distorted by your own cranium. To hear what others hear, you have to listen from the outside. Similar to the video example above, you can best achieve this with both a tape recorder and a mirror. The tape recorder, obviously, will give you a playback as to the tone, pitch, and speed of your speech. This helps you get a sense of how others hear you.

The mirror is a very revealing method of observing *how* you speak, since it allows you to see how your entire face as well as your hands and torso move as you speak. This is a surefire method of improving the timbre and the variety of your verbal communication, since anyone who observes himself speak will immediately and unconsciously seek to "brighten" his facial expression, which inevitably warms the tone of the voice. A warmer vocal tone delivers greater emotional connection with the other person and therefore adds greater depth and value to short telephone conversations, and long term relationships alike. It's one of the simplest and most useful pieces of advice I give to anyone who has to spend time on the telephone: Have a mirror nearby so you can see yourself speak. You cannot do much to change the physical structure of your vocal chords, of course, but there is a lot you can do to make them as influential as possible. Most of it has to do with slowing down.

If you find you speak fast, slow down. Not only does this make you easier to understand, it, too, lowers vocal tonality, both for men and women, which gives greater authority, presence, and influence. If you speak with an accent, do the same thing: Slow down. Accents add great variety to life and, in my opinion, should never be eliminated or suppressed. A far better and more impressive approach is to maintain an accent, but ensure it remains clear through slower, more considered speech.

People who make it their business to influence others constantly put this knowledge into practice. Great leaders think deeply and talk slowly. This allows them to take more time to convey a message, which, in a time-obsessed society, gives greater weight to the message itself. As with one's choice of image and dress, the choice of vocal pace also sets the tone of relationships. Fast talkers are perceived as nervous or perhaps slick. Agonizingly slow talkers can make people almost explode with frustration. But somewhere in between is the magic point where three powerful things happen.

- *You will be memorable.* The goal, in any conversation or meeting situation, is not only to be heard, but to be remembered, so that people act upon your suggestions or wishes. In a world of information overload, it is surprising just how powerful small things, such as a deeper, more soothing voice (for females and males alike) can be, when filtered through the emotional side of the listener's brain.
- *You will match the rhythm of the conversation.* Your conversation partners have a rhythm to their speech patterns, which reflects their ability to process and verbalize clear thought. Slowing down your speech creates an opportunity to listen for and pick up this natural rhythm and to match it, not beat for beat, but *slightly* slower, so that your spoken prose conveys even greater quality in comparison.
- *You will access the power of silence.* Talking slower makes it easier for silence to happen, and silence is a great conveyor of information. A pause allows a statement to add gravity to itself. Typically, the in-built momentum of normal conversational speech makes it easy—and certainly expected—for people to skip from one topic

to the next with little gap in between. There is a profound fear that silence may be mistaken for boredom or a derailment of the train of thought. But a pause, especially when reinforced by eye contact, helps to make a point. It allows time for the other person to think about what you've just said. The pause gives the listener permission to reflect upon it and to make mental notes. A pause also reinforces influence. Since many people are afraid of pauses, they will leap in to offer their thoughts or comments, simply to fill the gap and to end the silence. This can be of great strategic importance, given what it reveals about the other person, or of the position they are trying to assert. To pause and to let the other person speak first is to again maintain a true level of control within the organic relationship that is human conversation.

If such suggestions sound silly or excessive, listen to the recorded speeches, or sound bites, even, of truly great orators like Winston Churchill or Nelson Mandela. You will notice that a great deal of effort is expended in leveraging all natural oratorical gifts. They match the words they want to say with the rhythm that will best carry it, so that the message is most effectively delivered and the desired responses or actions are attained. Rhythm is an emotion-focused reaction, one of our most basic and ancient attributes, and it resides deep in the core of human perception. It sits there waiting to leveraged fully by those who know its power.

One of the best circumstances where this can be put into practice, and one of the least considered, is answering a phone. Once again, the reactionary nature of answering a phone call causes people to forget that an opportunity for influence exists. Let the phone ring one extra time. Pause briefly to clear your throat, and take a moment to center and deepen your voice by saying a few words slowly and quietly to yourself—almost like a quick prayer—before answering. Yes, it sounds strange and goes against our reactionary nature, but this, too, helps loosen the vocal chords and lower the vocal tone. Nobody questions opera singers when they sing their own warm-up parts. Why? Because it's an expected part of their role as a vocalist. It makes them credible as a performer. Well, you're a performer, too. A quiet, three-second warm-up is all you need to change your voice and your attitude from reactive to proactive, from ordinary to influential for the call you're about to take.

THE POWER OF WRITING

Although writing is secondary by far to face-to-face communication, it will always remain necessary. Consider the numerous forms of writing that people deal with daily, including memos, PowerPoint presentations, email, text messages, proposals, speeches, press releases, and many more. But many people tend to write in the same way they travel—event to event. In just the same way that traveling time and distance are seldom factored into a busy person's mental assessment of an upcoming day, the act of writing is, due to time pressure and the speed of the moment, reduced to a quick activity, a hasty spell-check, followed by a swift mouse click on either "Send" or "Print."

Don't dismiss the concept of poor writing as just meaning bad spelling and grammar. These are merely symptoms. All writing is an exercise in influence, and poor writing is that which fails to influence the reader in the manner you desire. What sort of influence? It might involve your reader buying your product or buying into your idea or simply attending your meeting. Influence might simply refer to the fact that your message gets read and attended to before all the other ones in a reader's inbox. As it is with the concept of meetings, the objective of any written communication is to pull more productivity or profitability out of a given situation. There must be a positive balance on the ergonomic balance sheet for the task to be worthwhile. In other words, the time it takes to write and send a message is time you can't get back. Your message must yield response or reaction in the reader that exceeds the value of the time you have invested. Many people simply write to get a task off their desk and out of their hair. That's the quick, but less effective way. It is quite easy to make your writing more effective, however. It doesn't require a degree in English literature, but it is best achieved by allowing enough time for planning beforehand and proofing afterwards.

Tips for More Effective Writing

- Include only one message per email/letter. Don't confuse your reader with two or more distinct messages. Only one will be remembered.
- Make sure your Subject Line completely summarizes your single message.
- Set up an agreement with your team to use prefixes in the subject line, such as [PJ] for "Project" so that they can set up their email rules to color all PJ messages in red, for greater visibility and quicker turnaround.
- Ask yourself what the intention of this message is, and what its payoff should be.
- Always write the most important single idea in the opening paragraph. Summarize it in the subject line.
- Use subsequent paragraphs to back up the main idea and make suggestions.
- Close off with an upbeat call to action—tell the reader what you want to have happen next.
- Allow time to proofread, spell-check, and grammar-check.

Planning Your Writing

Planning a written document, from a large presentation to the simplest email should not be an overly long exercise. It need take just a couple of minutes. What's important, however, is to ensure those minutes are given over to it, which can be quite a challenge in the high-speed world of event-to-event thinking. It should ensure that the true end result—the objective of the message—is known and is properly communicated. What is this "true end result"? It's not the moment at which the message is written and completed. The true end result is defined by what the reader does once having received and read it. All of your documents can be influential once you can answer these questions during your planning phase:

- What single message do I need to tell this reader?
- What action do I want from this reader?
- If I am responding, how will my response further the situation?
- If I am responding, what is the appropriate response time?
- What turnaround time should I expect once the reader receives my letter?
- What can I do/say to influence and improve that turnaround time?
- What tone do I need to adopt?
- How much detail do I need to include?
- What medium is the best for the context? Email? Phone? Face-to-face meeting?
- What will be my "hook" to grab the reader's attention? It can be as simple as a short, to-the-point subject line.
- What will be my call to action? How will I phrase it?

This may all sound very officious and obsessive for email, but the true end result speaks for itself: When your communication style stands head and shoulders above the style of everyone around you, people will gravitate towards it, and you will receive satisfaction more quickly. Your subject lines will grab attention; your calls to action will yield action. Your messages have to compete with many other sources of information that your reader must face every hour, perhaps every minute. It's up to you to ensure yours stand out, get noticed, and elicit the right type of response. It's like fishing on a river bank that's crowded with other anglers. You can hope your line gets noticed, or you can take a little time to walk upstream for a couple of minutes and enjoy unfettered access. Which do you think would yield the best results?

Proofing: Making Sure Your Writing Is Ready

Writing, just like personal appearance, needs proofing to be excellent. Event-to-event thinking allows people very little time to proof and correct their work, other than a rudimentary spell-check. Though most spell-checkers, and to some extent grammar checkers, catch the most obvious errors, they often overlook mistakes, and they are not able to refine the message's value. That's a human skill.

This poem, attributed to Guffey, Rhodes, and Rogin from their book *Business Communication: Process and Product*, highlights this fact simply and beautifully: It's fun to type this poem in your word processing program to observe how many errors the spell-checker detects:

> I have a spell checker
> That came with my PC.
> It plainly marks four my review
> Mistakes I cannot sea.
> I've run this poem threw it,
> I'm sure your pleased too no.
> Its letter perfect in it's weigh
> My checker tolled me sew.[1]

The best kind of proofing involves the use of two sets of eyes to review the written material, as well as a little time to do it.

- *New eyes.* When choosing two sets of eyes, the best approach is two sets of *different* eyes. For your most important writing, make sure they can be reviewed by someone else. Yes, this takes time, but the time it takes to proof now will always be less than the time it takes to correct later. Someone else's eyes will see the things you don't see—oversights, mistakes, awkwardness.
- *Fresh eyes.* If you only have yourself to work with, then fresh eyes are the next best approach. Even when composing the simplest email, if you take a moment to look away and do something else before sending, your refreshed eyes stand a better chance at top-quality proofing. This ties in with the distraction factor described in Chapter 2, except this time we *want* the distraction to happen. When you complete an email, before reaching for the Send button, move your eyes elsewhere: Find the files for your next task; get up and get some water or a snack; or simply look around the room or out the window, just for a few seconds. When your eyes return to the written text, the flow of concentration will have been broken. In

this case it's a good thing. For now, you will be able to review your work with reasonably fresh eyes. You will see errors that you didn't see before. You might even remember to attach the attachments as promised in the letter. This pause, this slowing down of the act of writing helps ensure that you are saying what you intended to say and that the end result will be what you want it to be.

THE POWER OF PERSONAL PROOFING

The idea of slowing down long enough to proof correctly doesn't apply just to the basic world of business writing. It also can be applied very successfully to you—a thinking, creative professional intent on furthering, or at least keeping your job and your lifestyle. For when searching for or working on a creative idea, one of the best ways of making it really great is to hear yourself speak the ideas out loud. This can best be achieved by allowing yourself time to slow down and talk to someone over coffee, perhaps, or lunch, or as mentioned earlier, during your commute. The first benefit gleaned from this technique is that your conversation partner might be able to offer her own comments and advice. But more important, when you hear yourself verbalize and externalize your own internal ideas, they become more real as you act as your own audience and critic.

The act of hearing yourself speak might seem excessive, even antiquated in the age of high-speed messaging, but in actual fact, in doing this you are leveraging a key technique for learning and creativity, which is similar to the procedure involved in creating a hologram. A hologram is an image made up of interference patterns created when two separate laser beams are bounced off an image or scene and are then redirected at each other and recorded on a glass plate. Holograms are intriguing in that they appear three-dimensional, and what they currently lack in color, they make up for in astonishing sharpness and clarity. The incredible thing about holograms is not just the three-dimensional image that you see when moving the holographic plate around, but also that if the plate were smashed, each broken piece would contain an entire copy of the hologram from the perspective of the piece's location on the original plate.

This is how many researchers who deal with knowledge and memory theorize how the brain might work. Though there is no one particular area of the brain reserved for long-term storage, it is thought that when fresh waves of information, in the form of experience, interact with stored factual fragments, an interference pattern gets created and that becomes the thing that we call knowledge.

Now it must be added that there are many theories in the field of cognitive psychology and neuropsychology about how the brain supposedly works. However, most point to this vast, yet subtle interaction between different areas of the brain—some of which are chemical and some electric—in which knowledge and other mental skills interact with each other at phenomenal speed. That is why it's so important to hear yourself speak. As your statements re-enter your brain by way of your ears, they interact with the slice of knowledge that originally created the idea, and create a kind of interpretation that is not only clearer, but deeper. There is more going on here than just "thinking it over." You are also hearing it anew. And that's something quite different. Can you find the time in your day to sit down with a colleague and "bounce your ideas" off him for a while? It will be worth more than wrestling the problem by yourself in silence.

THE POWER OF INFLUENCE THROUGH SELLING

When people think of selling, a common image that arises is that of the account executive, who has been schooled in cold-calling and spends most of his time hustling new business wherever he can find it. But really, all people are in sales in some fashion or other. It's just a matter of what's being sold. Salesmanship is not about moving widgets from one side of a counter to another. It's about establishing and building trust with an end customer. Trust is an intellectual and emotional resource, not a packaged good. People in non-sales jobs, such as administration, internal accounting, reception, and management are all in sales: They're selling ideas, image, motivation, communication, trust, and teamwork.

One of the primary reasons for writing this book, and for professing the value of *cooling down* in so many different areas of professional life is because I think the act of pulling your nose away from the grindstone is very important—your future employability demands it. Traditional sales-oriented professionals have always known the importance of hunting to survive, but this is not always the case for professionals in other vocations. Lawyers, for example, are able to solve problems, oversee procedures, and convince other people of their clients' cause. But in recent years, lawyers and the firms they work for have discovered that in order to secure new business in an increasingly competitive global world, they need to actually learn how to sell, and more and more it is up to the lawyers themselves, not the marketing department, to do this.

Similarly, physicians, whose approach to problem solving is scientific and rigorous, whose talents have traditionally focused on quick assessment and adherence to medical practices, may find themselves at a loss when it comes to selling, whether in terms of managing a practice, a department, or simply dealing with hospital executives. Many physicians are burning out and leaving their practices as a consequence.

Accountants and financial analysts have always been content to work quietly, diligently, and accurately. There are few extroverts in their field. But industries and economies change. An accountant need not become an extrovert to market her firm effectively. But if she is waist-deep in work and unable to clear her agenda until tax season has passed, she might be forced to stand by helplessly as business development opportunities for the quieter months pass her by. Selling need not be external and focused on business development. Consider the concept of internal, in-house selling. Take, for example, the frustration felt by someone who feels her manager has no idea of the amount of work she's putting in on a weekly basis and who only seems interested in talking about it when the annual performance review is due. Similarly, think about an individual who is trying to influence a group to listen to and accept his ideas during a meeting or teleconference, especially where change is involved. Or what about a busy person who desperately needs to give herself permission to close her office door and get some work done without upsetting her employees?

All of these professionals—the lawyers, the accountants, and the busy "inside" people—need to *cool down*, just enough to assess, develop, and refine new core skills that will enable them to continue practicing their respective crafts. There is a need for all professionals to know more about how to rebuild desire in the heart of their specific customers. But how do you do that? By understanding that building your future, on any level or scale, is based on how you sell these ideas. Sales is based on trust, and trust is obtained through slowing down.

Building Trust

When I work with people who actually work in sales, helping them develop more successful strategies for obtaining and retaining customers, one of the primary questions I get them to answer is this: "What differentiates you from all the other people in that company across the street?" Price is generally not their final answer.

What buyers of any product or idea truly seek is a good feeling, an emotional reassurance that conveys something more than just a transaction of goods for money. They require demonstrations of accountability, reliability, support, and security that allow them to feel less exposed and less at risk, both during the transaction, and more important, afterwards. The commodity that buyers truly seek is trust. Nobody has a monopoly on that.

Trust comes from slowing down, from taking the time to understand the buyer's needs and to illustrate to him how you address that need on many levels. This is true whether you are selling an actual widget or seeking to influence a senior manager or a colleague on a new initiative. Consequently, the best selling happens when it doesn't appear overtly but instead occurs through slow, careful assessments of the needs of the buyer. People who sell in this fashion still communicate with their customers, of course, but their conversations are more relaxed. Their objective is to allow the customer to lower his walls of defense. It's about hearing what the other person has to say and being able to offer a solution.

- *Lawyers and accountants.* For example, these professionals wish to enhance their firm's position in the marketplace need not learn aggressive sales skills. All they need to do is to network more, take some time to connect with other people, including non-lawyers and non-accountants, and practice the art of active listening (see next section, below). This can be a great challenge, given how much of a professional's formative years are spent racing the clock and handling overloaded schedules.

- *Physicians and other professionals.* Many doctors and others who practice by hourly appointment have learned, either the hard way or through education, the value of taking some time away from the practice—whether a single a day off or a year-long or a six-month sabbatical—not because it's nice (remember the opening line of this book)—but because it's essential to maintain a productive pace without falling ill or burning out. They need first to sell themselves on this idea, and then their colleagues, and finally their patients. Can they do it? What would be the alternative? Those who cannot sell in this manner may be setting themselves up for death-in-harness, and that does no-one any good.

- *Buying private time.* Let's say you work in an office with an open-door policy. You desperately need some time to close the door so you can get some work done, but you don't wish to alienate your employees. What do you do? By informing your staff that your door will never be closed for more than an hour, and keeping these closed-door periods to no more than two a day, you can build trust in the minds of the employees that their issues will still be answered and that you will still be available 80 percent of the day, and within a reasonable amount of time. It takes time to build and develop this habit, but the time taken wins you at least two hours of undisturbed work per day.

- *Building trust by being available.* You have a group of people assigned to you for a project. You have your own tasks to complete on this project, and you are already behind. What's the best way to ensure timely completion? Take the time to incorporate the practice of "management by walking around," (MBWA), a *slow* technique that requires that you leave your office and observe and interact with the people who report to you. Though this also takes time, it helps in two major ways that will ultimately speed up production: First it removes you from the Silo Effect generated by interfacing solely by email, and second it allows for greater interaction, in which the project's vision and status is shared and reinforced with the group, resulting in greater levels of enthusiasm, loyalty, motivation, and autonomy.

How to Sell While Appearing Not to Be Selling

- Go into a conversation with an agenda and an objective, but let them sit on the back burner of your well-prepared, *cool* mind, rather than stating them outright.
- Find a topic of mutual interest and base the conversation on that.
- Let the conversation veer towards the needs or problems of the other person.
- Practice and demonstrate active listening.
- Generate a genuine sense of trust and camaraderie by sympathizing or agreeing with the other person's statements.
- While doing this, formulate in your mind a plan as to how your objectives can best coincide with the other person's needs.
- Make mention of these possible solutions casually and gently.
- Observe the other person's body language, facial gestures, and eye contact and let these be your guide for further pacing.
- Seek to arrive at agreement.
- Before concluding the conversation, ensure that key points and agreements are repeated and clear.
- Identify next steps.
- After the conversation has concluded, *and before starting anything else*, write all of your thoughts and ideas down and schedule the follow-up activities.

ACTIVE LISTENING AND NEGOTIATION

Active listening basically comes down to the art of slowing down enough to allow the other person to do most of the talking in a conversation. People love to talk, especially about themselves. In a sales situation, any situation in which you wish to convince another human being to see things your way, the act of immediately charging ahead with benefit statements and compelling stories is superfluous and ill-timed. The best method for converting a prospect into a customer is to let her tell you what's wrong. For a cold-call situation, this means demonstrating genuine interest in the person to whom you are talking and asking more about her than what you're giving out about yourself. People will remember you as a fantastic conversationalist when you actually talk less and listen more. In a work situation, active listening means chatting with a manager or colleague about her problems and priorities first, even though your own priorities are just itching to get out.

Remember to avoid using the word "I." When a person tells you something about herself, the immediate reaction for most people is to reciprocate with a personal connection. For example, Mary says, "My boss just asked me to work over the weekend again." The common response might be, "I had to do that last week." Although appearing to demonstrate sympathy, such a statement moves the spotlight away from Mary and on to you. An active-listening response would be, "How do you feel about that?" or "What are you going to do?" To listen actively, minimize the use of "I" and maximize the use of "you."

Just look at this example, from Michael Gerber's excellent book, *The E-Myth Revisited*, which highlights the power of slowing down through active listening and creative problem solving rather than charging ahead with high-speed reaction:

> … what does the salesperson in a retail store invariably say to the incoming customer? He says, "May I help you?"… And how does the customer invariably respond? He says, "No, thanks, just looking." … Can you imagine what those few words are costing retailers in this country in lost sales?
>
> Instead of asking, "Hi, may I help you?" try "Hi, have you been in here before?" The customer will respond either with a "yes" or a "no." In either case you are then free to pursue the conversation.[2]

Gerber's proposed innovation demonstrates how easy it is to get past the defenses of anyone in any sort of "sales" situation and get straight on to progress. The overture is slower, yes, since any active-listening-based conversation takes longer to complete than making 10 cold calls or writing 10 impersonal emails. But this path to success, though slower in pace, is shorter. It's a classic example of getting further by going slower.

Here are some other practical applications of this concept.

Dealing with Multiple Tasks and Conflicting Priorities

This is a classic time-management problem in which the stress of overload confounds clear strategic thought. The fast approach is just to buckle down and try to get it all done, even if it means putting aside other tasks and coming in on the weekend to catch up. A *slow* approach might be to take more time to inquire about the task(s) being assigned, specifically, their deadlines. This does not mean asking for more time to complete the job, nor is it a challenge to the authority of the person doing the assigning. It is simply a classic component of project management in which vision is shared across a team. In this case, the onus may be upon you as the recipient of the task request to seek out the information, to learn more about the role this particular task has within a larger project timeline or within the requestor's own schedule. Once again, the key is to ask "you" questions rather than making "I" statements.

Managing Up

The term "managing up" demonstrates that selling can happen upwards, also. Managing up requires that you ask for more frequent opportunities to touch base and meet with your manager or other stakeholders. Meetings of this sort, which need not be overly long, allow for the opportunity to discuss future projects and timelines, and thus lay out more practical work times and delivery times in advance. In the case of two conflicting tasks, there may be many other suitable delivery times that will appease the requestor and work equally well. But without the use of this type of selling technique, there might not be any opportunity to discover them.

Delegation

Time-pressed business people seldom have the time or the patience to delegate. They live in the momentum of the moment. Yet support staff, colleagues, and subordinates are people who for the most part are eager and willing to learn new skills and take on new responsibilities. Such opportunities are often a primary reason for staying loyal to an employer: It's not just the money—it's the challenge. Support people can do great things, and in doing great things, can liberate you to realize even greater accomplishments. But true delegation, real assignment of tasks, and the establishment of trust take time.

Consider, for example, a commissioned salesperson, who, immediately after having had a great and productive conversation with a newly won client, then steps away from the phone to take care of the paperwork. Is this a good use of her time? It appears to be, since the paperwork has to get done, but would it not be more advantageous to get back on the phone—to strike while the iron is still hot? The energy and enthusiasm that come from making that great connection with a new customer should be immediately applied to connecting with another human being! To stop now is to let all that human excellence go cold, like pudding, and no-one wants to have to break through pudding skin to start over. But to leverage this type of momentum, the entrepreneur must slow down somewhere, just long enough to assess where and how the work that supports her business can be delegated. In this case she must sell to herself the idea that doing administrative work herself simply generates a false sense of busy-ness, which, at the end of the day amounts to far fewer sales.

How to Delegate Effectively

- First recognize that delegation is a slow act of education and trust, not a quick act of dumping.
- Allow time to seek out the right person for the job.
- Understand more about the people who work with/for you. Learn who is looking for or is ready for new challenges.

- Envision delegation as a three-step process. The first time you delegate a task, you are there to instruct and will therefore be doing all of the work anyway.
- The second time, you can expect a delegate to be able to complete the task to 50 percent satisfaction. Be prepared to schedule time to do the other half.
- The third time through, a delegate should be able to perform 75 percent of a task. Again, be prepared to schedule time to do the remainder.
- By the fourth time, a delegate should have both the skills and the confidence to complete the task almost to your own standards. Be sure to allow time to finish it off.
- This is hard work. But in the end you will have freed yourself up for more valuable tasks, and you will have created a more loyal and satisfied employee.
- If you have trouble deciding whether to delegate, remember two things: First perfection in others takes time. Second, just because you *can* do a particular task doesn't mean you *should* be doing it. Do you have the desire to slow down and assess the options?

THE POWER OF PLANNING

This section looks at the strategic advantages of *cooling down* enough to anticipate and even influence future events. The objective here, as with most of the chapters in this book, is to demonstrate the absolute value of slowing down in order to get further ahead. The school of project management, which I discussed in Chapter 5, strongly espouses the importance of thorough planning in advance of execution—something that is very difficult to do when under pressure and a quick, knee-jerk response appears preferable. Here are a few specific how-tos, each of which underscores the value of planning before acting.

PLANNING AHEAD

- *Assessing timelines.* Most things take longer than we want them to, but most of us plan too optimistically. This is why Parkinson's Law exists, and why rushing event to event exists. By taking the time to assess realistic timelines, you will be better able to face a realistic day. Even if crises are a regular part of your daily life, by expecting the crisis you remove its reactive, emotional power and turn it back into a regular task. When you schedule a phone call, how long do you think it should take? How long do you want it to take? Can you plan in your mind, before lifting the receiver, how long you will give the person on the other end? Can you inform that person, with correctly chosen, positive words, how long this call should take? When you say yes to a request from a colleague, are you assessing how long this task might take, or are you accepting it for fear of offending? Could you instead take a few minutes with that person and analyze the task together, including alternative timelines or other people to whom you could delegate? These are all small examples of taking the time in advance to identify and reify timelines before moving ahead.

- *Preparing for meetings.* Planning ahead is not reserved solely for tasks, of course. When the chairperson of a meeting chooses to slow down a little, he is then able to put more thought not just into the timing of the agenda items but also into the strategic seating of other participants around the table, so as to keep the jokers and the stronger personalities closer, and to maintain a line of sight with the quiet analytical types. This guarantees stronger and more equitable participation and, in turn, greater profitability for the meeting. By planning his entire day, so that he is not running from event to event, the chairperson ensures that he arrives first at the meeting. This allows him to set the stage physically. In addition to seating plans, he can ensure the room is appropriate, any technology to be used, e.g., projectors, teleconference phones, etc., are functioning, in fact, that everything will go smoothly. This helps set the stage emotionally for all participants and helps to focus the meeting from the very start.

- *Seating at restaurants or other discussion scenarios.* People in a hurry don't get much of a chance to contemplate the finer points of power within face-to-face relationships. Often, when they're running late and thinking event to event, it seems like a miracle just getting to the next appointment on time. This, of course, removes the possibility of maximum leverage. Take, for example, a two-person meeting. Whether it's at a restaurant or in a meeting room, the person who arrives first gets first pick of the seating. That opportunity profoundly influences the power relationship of the meeting from that point forward. Whoever arrives second must accept second choice. This principle applies regardless of gender or rank. For the person who arrives second, the territory has already been staked. This might make a big difference in the quality of the conversation and its ultimate profitability.

- *Knowing as much as possible before a meeting.* Knowledge is power, as many claim, and the more you have of it, the better suited you will be for a well-informed, productive interaction. This means taking the time to perform due diligence on a person or company prior to a first meeting. The information gleaned from this type of research can easily be reviewed during those quiet, clear moments between the time you arrive at the meeting place and the actual start of the meeting. It also refers to ensuring your pre-departure checklist is reviewed and complete, including exact knowledge of directions, cross streets, security access, and anything else that might serve to otherwise delay your arrival and raise your stress level.

Ultimately the act of turning yourself into a *cooler* person is a practiced skill that takes time to perfect, but one that can justify its investment through improved relationships, improved influence, and heightened productivity. It is essential to remember that as human beings we must constantly battle against instincts and emotions that make the quick route more attractive. How often have you found yourself cursing a situation because of speed? A driver cuts you off, a printer jams, a cell phone cuts out. Anger is a high-speed autonomic defense reflex, but as I demonstrated in earlier chapters, it comes at great cost to the human body and to relationships. People have long memories when it comes to vivid, angry outbursts.

Anger embodies the dangers of speed and is the antithesis of *cool*. To conclude, I'd like to share another story, a parable of sorts, taken from the famous "Kansas City Story." There is no better example of the cost of speed.

A chief executive who sent his staff an email accusing them of being lazy and threatening them with the sack has seen the share price of his company plummet after his message was posted on the Internet.

In the three days after publication of his outburst—which gave managers a two-week ultimatum to shape up—stock in the American health care company dropped by 22 percent over concerns about staff morale. It is now trading at more than a third less than it was before the email was sent.

His email to managers read: "We are getting less than 40 hours of work from a large number of our employees. The parking lot is sparsely used at 8 a.m.; likewise at 5 p.m. As managers, you either do not know what your employees are doing or you do not care. In either case, you have a problem and you will fix it or I will replace you."

... The CEO wanted to see the car park nearly full by 7:30 a.m. and half-full on weekends. He wrote: "You have two weeks. Tick, tock."

A week later, the email appeared on a Yahoo financial message board and Wall Street analysts began receiving calls from worried shareholders.[3]

KEY POINTS TO TAKE AWAY

- Knowing what you look like reinforces the idea that human beings access 70 percent of what they know by way of visual cues and non-verbal communication.
- Knowing what you look like enhances charisma and influence.
- Knowing what you sound like is as important as knowing what you look like in terms of making you appear more relaxed, credible, and influencial.
- Writing requires a discipline and a style that connects to the reader and motivates him to action.
- Top-quality writing is achieved by planning and proofing.
- The "true end result" refers to what the reader does once having received and read an email communication (or any other type of communication). Are you able to slow down enough to identify the true end result?
- Hearing yourself speak is a powerful way of assessing your own ideas.
- Selling and influencing others are skills that every person needs. They are based on active listening and trust.
- Managing up and delegation are two examples of how time and focus on others can yield greater results for you.
- We can learn the value of planning from professional project managers, and then apply their proven techniques to all situations.

HOW TO *COOL DOWN*

Image

- How do you come across to others?
- How do you know? Who have you asked?

How Do You Sell?

- What is your job? In what ways do you "sell" in order to get your work done?
- Who do you talk to?
- Who do you try to impress? How many people do you need to sell to and on how many levels?
- Analyze your current techniques for connecting with the people you wish to influence. How much "telling" do you do? How much "listening"?
- What differentiates you from all the other "suits" in the company across the street?
- Are your clients aware of what makes you different?
- Have you asked them? Have they told you?
- What techniques are you willing to try so you can observe your visual and speaking skills?

Active Listening

- How good are your active listening skills?
- Do you find you prefer to talk about yourself more than the other person when you're in a conversation?
- What's the one concept about you that you would want a prospect (internal or external) to take away with them?

Managing Up

- Do you have a strategy for managing up? What is it?
- What kind of manager do you work for?

- How accepting of managing up do you think your manager will be?

Delegation

- How comfortable are you with delegating tasks to others?
- Do you have access to mentors who could help teach you the art of delegation?
- Are you willing to invest the time to learn how to delegate using the four-step process in which the "student" takes a little more responsibility for his new skill with each step, but in which you must budget sufficient time to oversee each step?
- Have you have any experience with delegation? Many people dislike delegation because of a bad experience in which they "dumped" a task on someone who was truly unprepared.
- Are you willing to invest the time to learn how to delegate using the four-step process?

Dealing with Anger

- How do you deal with anger?
- The old adage rings true: count to 10 and take deep breaths. This infuses the brain with additional oxygen that allows the anger reflex to subside. It gives you time to ask the question: "What will this issue (that is making me angry) mean to me a year from now?" This usually helps keep anger-inducing situations in perspective.

Orators

- Who do you consider a great orator? Why?
- How do you rate your own skills at speaking? What are your perceived weaknesses? Fears? What do others say about your speaking skills? Have you asked them?
- Where is your local Toastmasters chapter? Have you ever visited? Toastmasters is a valuable resource for learning to speak and present

clearly. I strongly recommend that people visit a local chapter at least once. Information about Toastmasters can be found at www. toastmasters.org.

1 Guffey, Mary Ellen, *Business Communication: Process and Product.* South-Western College Pub; 4th edition (March 11, 2002).
2 Gerber, Michael, *The E-Myth Revisited: Why Most Small Businesses Don't Work and What to Do About It.* Collins; Updated edition (April 12, 1995).
3 "Boss's e-mail bites back," quoted in BBC World News, April 6, 2001, http://news.bbc.co.uk/2/hi/americas/1263917.stm

FEAR GRIPS THE BODY.

IT PARALYZES THE SOUL

AND PULLS BLINDNESS IN.

CHAPTER 8 FEAR

One of the most significant human talents to have been drowned out by the noise of high-speed culture is that of being able to confront fear. Fear, as we all know, is an emotional reaction, based on a sense of imminent danger to the self. Because of its emotional nature, our primary reactions to fear are reflexive and not necessarily logical.

For those interested in adopting *cool* methods, fear stands as a major obstacle, since implementation means initiating change. Change represents an unknown element, and unknown elements spark fear. None of this is particularly welcome to the human body and mind, of course, and the result is resistance. When all of this occurs within the swirling ocean of external stimuli it becomes a lot easier, on the whole, to bypass the whole issue and stick with the status quo and stay close to the grindstone, secure in the harness.

I have worked with thousands of people who have looked with awe at the new possibilities that *cooling down* offers, even down to something as simple as daring to run a meeting more effectively. For a brief moment, their eyes sparkle with promise until, quickly, the spark of innovation is extinguished by fear, and their eyes and expression regain their grim air of conviction.

FEAR OF LOSING YOUR JOB

The number one reservation, of course, is the fear that rocking the boat will result in you falling overboard: that any suggestions of improvement, especially that include the word *slow* will end up a career-limiting move. How could anyone expect to question the way work is done around here? How can you question the boss about anything? How can you dare to introduce the word *slow* into any work-related discussion without risking repercussions? In virtually all organizations the spoken or unspoken expectation is for quick turnaround, high productivity, and the willingness to work in a multitasking environment. The mantra is "just get it done." That being the case, why would anyone want to stick her neck out to introduce the four-letter word *slow*? After all, there's always someone else who could take the work, someone else ready to do your job.

Fear is something to be faced and conquered. It must never be allowed to rule, although it tries very hard to do just that. In spreading its contagious message, fear relies on speed as its co-conspirator. Speed can make people react too quickly and can make them do the wrong things. Speed makes people procrastinate by offering all sorts of distractions and thought-occupiers that both magnify the fear and encourage avoidance of the problem.

Write It Out

The problem with fear is that it exists primarily in the mind. It sloshes around in the short-term "working" memory, amorphous yet painfully present. To handle fear, it is necessary to remove it from its lair and expose it to the open air—to get it on paper.

Nothing quells fear and spurs creative thought better than getting thoughts—even negative ones—down on paper. Some people like to write free-form—just paragraph after paragraph of flow-of-consciousness text. Others use bullet points to separate problems from solutions. Others set their fears out in a columnar format like the one below:

The Issue	The Worry	The Resolution
Slowing down will get my boss mad at me.	My boss might fire me or reduce my bonus.	What is my boss's perspective? Set up a time to chat?

As I mention in a couple of places in this book, addressing fear in this manner works because revisiting your own ideas by rereading them or even hearing them is an exercise in cognitive reprogramming; it helps put them into clearer perspective by using the logical side of the brain rather than leaving them in the constant ethereal swirl typical of the emotional side.

This, then, is another benefit of *slow*. People who take the time to write out their thoughts recognize a number of benefits:

- In times of heightened stress, the time you take to write out what's bothering you and to look over your notes helps remove you from the urgency of the moment, thus reducing your blood pressure and cooling your mind.
- The ideas, as we have seen, get reassessed and consciously reprioritized.
- There is also the tangible pleasure of the act of writing itself. This should never be overlooked. I have consciously used the word "writing" in this section because it offers significant sensory advantages to keyboarding in this context. Although it is certainly possible to list fears and issues on the screen of a computer, there is a distinct benefit in writing with ink, slowly and carefully, on good paper, that contributes significantly to the therapeutic benefits of this exercise. This highlights another human element lost to the age of speed that needs to be won back: Time to write things out.
- People who do this soon realize that the fear inherent in a particular situation truly is, as the acronym goes, a False Expectation Appearing Real. Human beings are remarkably adept at handling trying situations, once the demon of fear has been exorcised.

Communicate It

If the fear of losing your job is holding you back, I would ask you to think about the principles embodied in a well-known book, the *Art of War* by Sun Tzu. The friction between you and any other person in your life is akin to battle, even if on a small scale or even if no acrimony is remotely evident. Friction is a part of life and as such the principles taught by a master of "applied friction," such as Sun Tzu, are worth considering. The *Art of War* is not a book about rushing into conflict headlong and without due preparation. It's about victory through the principles of *slow*. For example, the battle in this case is between you and your manager. The prize being fought over is your job. The energy involved is fear. Sun Tzu would state that as with all battles, victory goes to the person who can recognize his enemy's strengths and weaknesses as well as his own, and who can strategize a means of attack or counterattack. In terms of the manager-employee relationship, the weapons of this battle are communication and influence rather than spears or muskets. Specifically:

- How well are you communicating your value statement? How proactive are you being in terms of communicating with your manager to let her know the types of tasks you are working on? Are you managing up sufficiently to ensure a level of up-to-date understanding?
- How active is your internal networking strategy? Are you meeting and talking regularly with team members, mentors, and suppliers?
- How are you demonstrating your personal value and vibrancy in a way that will help set you apart from your internal or external competitors?

Have you allowed the time for these proactive maneuvers, or are you too busy working too fast on today's immediacies?

FEAR OF OFFENDING THE CLIENT

The second major fear to be faced when thinking about working more coolly has to do with the customer or client. How on earth can anyone dare to go slow when the client is waiting?

Isn't prompt service, after all, the *lingua franca* of successful business? Isn't that what defines customer service?

Many will agree that speed is good, but speed can only be good when it's paired with quality. Even for those who serve fast food at a drive-through window, customer satisfaction will be attained only if the order being speedily delivered is the right one.

As we have seen, customers base their buying relationships on trust, not just price or speed. Yet many professionals in many industries, caught up in their own vortex of self-imposed hastiness, sometimes forget what it's like to stand in a customer's shoes.

- Financial people such as mortgage specialists, real estate agents, and insurance agents, might believe they are doing their clients a favor by helping them rush through the paperwork. In the process they may forget how overwhelming it is for the average consumer to sign so many unfamiliar documents that mean so much. They might forget that their ticket to repeat business and referral from a customer might be found through a distinctive combination of accuracy, empathy, and time.

- On-the-road salespeople might feel they can get more done if they fill their agenda with an overly optimistic number of calls and then drive like crazy to meet them all. But if they arrive unprepared, or at a time that is inconvenient to the customer, where does the value statement go?

- Similarly, people who visit their clients or whose clients visit them feel a great temptation to squeeze in one extra appointment out of fear of losing a new potential customer. But not all customers react positively to being squeezed in. Some would prefer to wait. Often, the best restaurants are those that only take reservations and even turn away last-minute arrivals. What is the reaction of someone who is turned away? A little humiliated, perhaps, but will it diminish her desire to dine there? Unlikely. It will probably increase it. The clients of high-prestige professionals such as doctors and lawyers expect to have to wait and would most likely be unnerved if their lawyer or doctor answered her own phone before the second ring. Exclusivity, the epitome of *cool*, methodical access, has panache, and from the standpoint of the human observer who judges by emotion first, *panache* speaks loudly and positively.

- What about voice mail? Many people express the legitimate fear that letting callers go to voice mail will result in trouble. "My customers will just go to our competitors," they say, or "They'll go to the switchboard and get someone to find me," or "They'll just escalate to my boss, and then I'll get in trouble." This concept was first addressed in Chapter 2, in the case study of *Mary's Interruptions and the Escalation Factor*, in which it was suggested that Mary refine her strategy regarding managing up in order to allow more time to discuss with her manager the value of her work and the reason for using voice mail. Now let's take that concept further.

In all four of the situations above, I believe it necessary for any working person to take the time to see the relationship through the customer's eyes. As we have already seen, the needs of most customers can be dealt with by giving them an alternate time at which calls will be returned, either within the hour, within the half-day, or by the end of business today. It is possible to satisfy callers, first by way of a substantive outbound greeting that informs them as to when they can expect a response and next by following up on that promise at the appointed time.

Not convinced? Do you still think that being *cool* in this fashion—that is to say, waiting until you're finished one important task before taking calls from your clients—might result in losing customers? Then write it out. Take a moment to answer the following questions:

- In what way do I fear my actions will offend my customer?
- What is my customer expecting of me?
- Why does the customer do business with me in the first place?
- What do I believe will drive the customer away?
- What can I do to counteract this?
- Have I recently taken the time to ask my customers these questions?

Once you have finished answering these questions, call up your manager and ask her for a meeting to talk about them. This combined technique of writing, thinking, discussing, and hearing yourself discuss the issues, will paint a clearer picture of what truly distinguishes you from your competition and how you can best satisfy the needs of your customers. This is a solid technique for banishing fear and replacing it with certainty.

Why Do People Read Books?

Here is an analogy that will help explain the value of using *slow* and tangible methods to confront fear and to ultimately ensure the vibrancy and longevity of your relationships with your customers. Think for a moment about why people still buy books: There is a value in the concept of "the tangible" that cannot be matched by high-speed replacements.

When the Internet started to flourish in the late 1990s many pundits declared the age of the paper book to be over, and they quickly welcomed the e-book as its replacement. They also declared how the paperless office would soon eliminate the need for excessive paper usage through the advent of on-screen media. But the lightning-quick e-book has not yet established any sort of firm foothold on the reading public, and currently more paper, not less, is being used in the offices and classrooms of the world. Certainly there have been changes in the book retail industry: Small, family-owned bookstores have been swallowed for the most part by big-box chains, yet people are still flocking to bookstores to buy books, and they're still printing out their PowerPoint presentations and Word documents by the millions.

Humans enjoy the look and feel of books, their design and layout, and most importantly, they enjoy, on an unconscious level, the way the brain processes printed material. Though there are e-books available, most consumers prefer to hold a paperback in their hands. And when it comes to important documents, a majority of business people will say that when they need to read them closely, they prefer the hard copy. Perhaps the greatest testament to the ongoing value people place in the opportunity to get lost in a good book are those millions of people of all ages who in recent years have willingly lugged around their hefty copies of *Harry Potter* in hardback.

What does all of this have to do with fear? Emotional stability comes largely from a connection to the tangible, which itself can only best be realized through *slow*. When people meet face to face, they learn more. When people plan out their actions, they do more. When they write out their fears, they solve more. You do not need to be a Hogwarts grad to master that type of magic.

FEAR OF BEING OUT OF THE LOOP

Chapter 2 also discusses the Loop—that mode of existence that so many high-speed people claim never to want to leave. The point of the Chapter 2 section was to highlight its existence and to suggest its implicitly self-destructive bias. Now I would like to look at that fear: the fear behind being left out of the loop. Every week a new study comes out that shows that increasing numbers of people choose not to take their allotted vacation time, or if they do take it, they continue to check in regularly to get their email and stay informed. This fear of being left out of the loop is so profound and widespread that there are holiday hotels that promote among their services the offer to lock guests' wireless tools in the vault for the duration of their stay. Is this addiction to work due to the fact that work is so continually interesting, or is it based on fear of being left out?

We could imagine this analysis being played out in an updated version of the TV special, *A Charlie Brown Christmas*, in which Lucy sits at her psychiatrist's booth, facing her client, Charlie Brown, who holds his PDA close to his chest as he speaks[1]:

Charlie Brown: "I can't stand it. Every time I think I can take a day away from my chores, I have to keep looking at this thing." (He looks at his wireless PDA.)

Lucy: "Hmmm. Maybe your problem is rooted in a deeper fear. Do you think you have a fear, Charlie Brown? If you have a fear of neglecting duty or responsibility, you have *paralipophobia*. If you have a fear of sitting still, you have *cathisophobia*. Or do you fear being forgotten? If you fear being forgotten you have *athazagoraphobia*."

Charlie Brown: (Leaping up from his stool, but not letting go of his PDA.): "That's it!"

A Counseling Example

I ask the people I work with and coach privately a series of questions. These questions are not intended to prove that there is one single approach to work and one single schedule that everyone must follow. The role of the questioning, as with much in the world of analysis and therapy, is an exercise in slowing down. During our sessions, the client herself can hear her own statements. No longer drowned out by the emotional rush of pressure and speed, she can therefore judge them more objectively.

- I ask a client what would happen if she were out of the loop from say 7:00 p.m. to 7:00 a.m. (supper and sleep time). Would her business collapse? Would she lose her job? Sometimes the answer to this question is "yes," or more precisely "yes, I think so." More often, though, the answer is a reluctant "no."
- I ask her to elaborate on how any potential job loss might happen and who is in charge of making it happen.
- I ask her what her definitions of her role are.
- I ask her how closely her definitions of her roles coincide with the definitions her manager has of them, and when they last checked in with each other on this issue.
- I ask her to state how long she plans to stay in this position, and what her mental, emotional, and career-oriented breaking points might be.
- Most important, I ask her to write down my questions and her answers.

It's fair to say that certain jobs are different, and there are requirements particular to each. If a client's job requires her to be on call for certain periods, that's fair enough. Maybe a lot of business gets done on Mondays and Tuesdays between 4:00 p.m. and 10:00 p.m. But for those clients who profess to be on call all day and night every day of the year, I ask them openly: What is driving this level of expectation, this willingness to put in a superhuman amount of on-call duty? Is it the company? The job? The boss? Or is it fear?

The Cost of Globalization

Sometimes the fear of being out of the loop is not internally driven but actually has its roots in the external world, specifically the global business world, where clients, suppliers, and co-workers from different hemispheres and time zones demand attention. It doesn't even have to be a "global" thing. Many North American workers struggle with the logistics of satisfying the needs of their colleagues on both coasts of their own country. When I see companies with global time allocation problems of this sort, I ask to see their standards manual or time zone policy. Usually they don't have one. And that reminds me of the good old days when email was just a pup.

When email technology was unleashed upon the world in the mid- to late-1990s, very few companies had any sort of operations guidelines. They were quick to legislate rules regarding personal use, the dissemination of confidential material, as well as a ban on pornographic and other hostile content, of course. But they offered very little guidance as to how the medium should be used.

To this day, there are hundreds upon hundreds of organizations that have not established comprehensive email policies. Nor have they quantified the cost, in dollars, hours, and productivity, that an underdeveloped email policy has wrought. The simplest example of this was described in Chapter 1, in which we saw how so many knowledge workers spend their prime productivity time responding to emails simply because they are there. To me that's like parking your car on the office flowerbed simply because it's closer to the door. Any company that has a global reach in terms of clients and/or suppliers needs to find the time to implement a time-zone strategy that ensures top-quality service from its head-office staff. That's obvious, of course. But let's look at an example.

Case Study: Time Trials

Joe works for ABC Company based in Boston. He puts in a full day of work and tries to get home by 6:00 or 7:00 p.m. most nights. The problem is, ABC's West Coast office has recently downsized some of its staff, and as a consequence, Joe has been assigned to take care of the needs of this team. Joe knows that every night he will receive two or more calls from the West Coast, since 8:30 p.m. on Joe's watch is only 5:30 p.m. Pacific time. Joe says he doesn't mind this, as he considers it to be part of his job, but he is starting to resent the imposition upon his personal time.

Given what you've learned about the chemistry of sleep and *presenteeism*, what might the prognosis be for Joe's ability to maintain top-level service both in the Boston office and for his colleagues in the West?

My feeling is the prognosis is poor. Sooner or later Joe will make a mistake and will have to pay for it. He is acting out of the fear of being left out of the loop in conjunction with an imposed expectation that he will answer these coast-to-coast calls.

My suggestion would be for him and his manager to draw some time maps. I suggest that he create an image that tangibly highlights the optimum overlaps of time that will ensure that the needs of the West Coast office can be met without requiring Joe to stay awake until midnight. This approach requires compromise, but more importantly, it will help influence and guide the actions of the West Coast team, to know that, with the exception of true emergencies, a distinct envelope of time exists for live communication.

Such a technique might not please everybody fully, and that's where a lot of the fear comes in. But what it will do is to draw up an accepted and understood plan of operations. This will help dissolve the fear of the loop and replace it with clearer, more productive thought.

The Achilles Heel of the U.S. Dream Team

The fear of being out of the loop, and the resultant desire to answer emails and other surface-level messages at any time of day or night puts the vast productivity potential of the North American workforce at a profound disadvantage precisely at the point in world history when it needs depth and creativity more than ever.

How to Prevent Superficial Attitudes from Creeping into the Workplace Culture

- First, recognize that such a danger exists. Recognize that speed generates a greater potential for complacency and error.
- Take a page from the world of project management in which all actions require closure: Allow time to review key activities, to perform post-mortems or debriefs before moving ahead. Track both positive and negative developments as they happen.
- Practice Management by Walking Around (MBWA) and empower others to do the same. No one knows better the advantages and disadvantages of a system (or its replacement) than the people on the front line.
- Quantify the current culture of fear in your workplace. What are you afraid of? What are other people afraid of? What is being done to make these fears tangible so that they may be confronted?
- Allow time to review what competitors and the marketplace are doing. Check with mentors. Observe and communicate new pest practices.
- Remember the old phrase: There is only one way that a person (or company) can coast, and that is downhill.

To illustrate this, observe Thomas Freidman's analysis of the U.S. Basketball "Dream Team" of the 2004 Olympic Games from his book, *The World Is Flat*.[2] This was the team that was trumpeted as the Goliath of the Games. It consisted of physically huge, talented, and experienced players from what was supposed to be the best, most powerful, and certainly the richest basketball league in the world, the NBA. Yet they were trounced by countries such as Puerto Rico, Lithuania, and Argentina. Their defeats were made more humiliating by the players' international celebrity. It was a fiasco.

What went wrong? Freidman argues that the attitude of the NBA had changed over time from a team sport in which players drilled on team plays, which included strategy, planning, and a certain degree of anonymity, to one in which the sole important factor was the individual's way-cool lay-up or the nothing-but-net dunk. In other words, they went for the basketball equivalent of the sound bite or photo-op: fast, intense, and impressive, but lacking the substance of a winning strategy.

If corporations, Freidman says, could remember failures of this nature, in which the strategy for victory ends up being based on the superficial and in which the energies of players end up being used for short-term turnaround of strategically insignificant components, then they might be able to foresee and avoid their own demise. This, I believe, applies to people like Joe and to the people who employ him as well as to all the companies and individuals who believe their own star status when it comes to staying in the loop. By assigning Joe the responsibility of taking all calls, his employers opted for a superficial solution: one that seems to solve the problem, but instead sets the stage for error and failure, which might still take management by surprise. Whether due to fatigue, overload, or error, more and more companies are going to start losing more and more games to upstart teams from lesser-known countries. That's a big price to pay.

FEAR OF SAYING NO

Next on people's big list of fears is that of simply saying no, whether to the boss, to a client, or to a colleague. This fear predates the advent of high-speed technology, of course, but it has certainly been compounded in an age where it is not only quicker and easier to avoid having to negotiate, but one in which people have lost the ability and the know-how to do just that. It's a lot easier to simply say, "Put it on my desk; I'll get to it when I can," or "Send me an email on that."

"No" is a bad word. We were taught its negative connotations way back when we were infants. But those who take the time to investigate the value of a *cool* approach will recognize that "no" comes in shades, not just black and white. There is room for negotiation under the canopy that stretches between yes and no; there is a mutually acceptable mid-ground. But finding it is a practiced art. If using no in your answer, you must factor in the necessary footholds that allow a requestor to accept your response.

Footholds for Negotiation

When confronted with a request, what are the alternatives to yes? Could you:

- Negotiate to do the task at a later time?
- Suggest a different person who might be able to take it on?
- Offer to do part of the task instead of all of it?
- Offer to trade one task for another?
- Assist the requestor in locating possible alternate solutions?

Could you negotiate for any of these alternatives, or do they seem too confrontational, too uncomfortable? This is the type of skilled human interaction that the age of email has eroded. How many of us, after all, are comfortable with haggling task for task, face to face? Very few.

The objective of this section is to state firmly that a yes without reservation does nothing but condition the requestor to expect the same deal every time. It sets the stage for a moral debt of servitude that compounds an already crowded day. And that's not healthy.

Case Study: Could You Say No to This Person?

Alan comes by your desk and drops a folder in front of you. He puts on a pained and helpless expression. "This is a copy of my report to the Development Committee," he says, "I just need you to proofread it, maybe add a little bit to the recommendations, you know—your usual magic. But I do need it back by 11:00. That's when the committee is meeting." It's currently 9:15 a.m. What do you do?

If I were the person approached by Alan, here's what I would *not* do. I would not say "no" to him outright. After all, he is a co-worker. Even though he's in the wrong in expecting me to drop everything at such short notice, I will still have to work with him on a daily basis.

But assuming none of the footholds for negotiation outlined in the list above is possible, what then? If I were to say yes, without reservation,

I would be conditioning Alan to know that he could make the same request again, at any time. That wouldn't be good.

So what I *would* do is this: I would use the power of *slow* to think through a better solution. "I will do this proofreading for you, Alan," I would say, "but my price is 15 minutes of your time, for a follow-up meeting, this afternoon."

The objective of this 15-minute meeting would be to discuss a more appropriate approach to the planning and proofing of his documents. Perhaps, if Alan needs me to play a part in his future projects, I can get him to agree to give me a minimum 24-hours' notice. I do not intend to scold or belittle Alan by doing this, but I do need to demonstrate to him that time is money, and my time, just like my money, is not something I give away freely. I intend to remove any preconception of my unlimited ability and replace it with an understanding, a business relationship.

Such is the strategic value of *slow*. The meeting will require 15 minutes from my afternoon. But that *slow* interlude will allow for a better use of my time whenever Alan and I need to work together again, and will likely reduce the number of times he asks for favors. If I had been too preoccupied with my wireless PDA at the time of his initial request, I would have set myself up for years of similar last-minute requests, with no-one to blame but myself.

The Bag of Guilt

I have met many people who have sought different ways to handle the guilt or frustration they feel for either saying no—or for *not* saying no. Some will try to dilute the sensation of guilt by taking home a loaded briefcase full of work that either didn't get done during the day because they took on additional requests, or full of new work that they took on out of an inability to say no. This briefcase travels home with them, full, but it does not get opened. It sits overnight full of work and returns next day to the office, still full of work. Somewhere in the act of carrying this extra burden, the briefcase owner derives a certain liberation, as if by carrying the work to and from his home he alleviates the guilt he would feel if he left the work behind at the office.

I applaud these people for not allowing work to chronically take over their home lives. I applaud the fact that once both the briefcase and its owner arrive home, the pleasure of home takes over and the briefcase stays in the hall—full, fat, and no longer important. The fact that it comes back the next day in the same condition, while its owner continues to hold her job, to do well on the annual review, to get bonuses, and to be seen as a team player is testament to the fact that much of what we do at work can wait.

Vicariously Living Out Our Fears

In my previous book, *Cool Time*, I mentioned how I believed the success of the various "Survivor" shows on television was due in large part to the cultural era of *schadenfreude* in which we now live. *Schadenfreude* is a German word meaning "taking pleasure in the misfortune of others," as happens each time a tribe member is booted off the island or an apprentice is fired. Our collective sense of powerlessness that comes from being so time-stressed requires an outlet, and reality TV provides the perfect venue. Why else is so much camera time given to the reactions of the losers at the moment of their ultimate humiliation? If the shows were just about adventure, the losers would not be shown to such a degree. But that's not the case. We need to see them suffer in order to feel better about ourselves.

It seems now that these *schadenfreude* shows are evolving, continually keeping pace with the frustrations felt in real life by their viewers. A cooking show, for example, features a superstar chef who explodes with rage and actually assaults his hapless interns with the very food they're trying to prepare. Through this exercise, we viewers can experience vicariously the type of "no" we would really like to say, or perhaps the reactions that we fear might come our way if we ourselves were to use that word.

People have been throwing Christians to the lions in one form or another for thousands of years. It would be incorrect to attribute the success of these *schadenfreude* shows exclusively to the fears and frustrations of high-speed life, but I think their huge popularity can be attributed in part to the motivations and tensions that we all experience.

How to Foster Creativity in Your Workplace

- Given that fear of slowing down is the greatest obstacle to encouraging creativity, the first step is to recognize that creative thought, experimentation, and blue-skying are not excuses to get away from work but opportunities to develop new innovations. In other words, eliminate the fear of silence and view it as action in its own right.
- Identify patterns in the work week or month in which time could be assigned to creative activities without losing out on current productivity opportunities. Is mid-month quieter than month-end, for example? Are Fridays before long weekends as busy as a typical Tuesday?
- Create a "war-room" or creativity room in which ideas can be shared visually on wall charts and other devices. This not only acknowledges and reinforces creative behavior, it also allows for a meeting of minds, where synergy can truly happen.
- Ensure that senior management participate in creativity exercises. Give workers concrete knowledge that management is behind them. Eliminate the fear that may be holding other staff members back from innovation.
- Adopt a policy by which each staff member can qualify to use a certain percentage of company time for tinkering. Consider that this was how a number of major inventions (such as 3M's Post-It note) happened.

THE FEAR OF EMPTINESS

The final fear to consider here is that of emptiness, the idea that space or time with nothing in it is somehow wasted, that continuous stimulation is the pulse of society. Fear of emptiness is natural. It stems from the fear of the unknown, one of the most primal of all fears. Fear of emptiness fuels our desire for constant stimulation, and the electronic world obliges.

But emptiness is not to be feared. Natural apprehension can be consciously overruled without the need to become a monk or a hermit.

- In Chapter 2, I highlighted the power of the seven-second silence as a key tool for eliciting creativity from people.
- In Chapter 5, I described the value of staring at your shoes during an elevator ride, staring at your coffee in the coffee shop, and staring out of the window during the train ride. All are examples of emptiness that yield great fullness.
- In Chapter 7, I addressed the concept of active listening, which refers to the art of staying quiet in order to allow your conversation partner to do most of the talking.

These are all examples in which emptiness yields greater power.

People fear emptiness in action. Busy-ness, it seems, satisfies the desire to feel busy. But what if you were allowed, as part of your job, to not be busy, at least for a while? What if you were allowed to tune out, to doodle, to think with no outside distraction? What might come of it?

The Ben Franklin Forum on Innovation, presented by Knowledge@ Wharton, at the University of Pennsylvania, describes the well-documented retreats that Microsoft founder Bill Gates is famous for taking every year at his cottage in Washington State. His strategy has allowed Microsoft to stay "a giant with a market capitalization of nearly $300 billion... [yet]...it retains the agility of a startup when it comes to introducing new products and improving old ones."[3] Imagine. The world's richest businessman, with so much pressure and so many things to occupy his time allowing himself to disappear and think like that.

The Wharton School forum also cites this example. "After becoming boss of Xerox in 2001, Anne Mulcahy wanted to pump up that company's innovative abilities even as she pared away costs. She sought out the advice of one Xerox researcher responsible for a large number of patents. 'He said that most innovation happens by accident and experiment, not design,' she recalled in a recent speech at Wharton. 'It's allowing people to push barriers.'"[4]

The thinkers at Wharton don't advocate that people wander around aimlessly, of course, but they do suggest strongly that a structure be put in place that encourages creativity. And this is another place where the benefits of *cooling down* become tangible. To me, the poster child for this type of approach still remains 3M, with its policy of encouraging their staff to spend 10 percent of their time tinkering, experimenting, and generally blue-skying. Just such an approach was eventually responsible for the invention of the Post-It note.

Fear of any sort is not to be feared. It is a reaction, and as such can be anticipated and refined. Fear is a living thing. It feeds on speed, and it is contagious. But the good news is it can be starved if people take the time to cut off its supply. And the best news of all is the opposite state of fear, that of being calm and cool, is also contagious, and equally abundant—yours for the taking.

KEY POINTS TO TAKE AWAY

- One of the most significant human abilities to have been drowned out is the ability to confront fear.
- You can deal with the fear of losing your job first by writing out your fears and their resolutions and identifying your value statement.
- The act of writing out thoughts, ideas, and worries is a powerful antidote to fear.
- The *Art of War* is not a book about rushing into conflict headlong and without due preparation. It's about victory through the principles of *slow*.
- The fear of offending the client can be countered by reinforcing the relationship through trust and time.
- People read books and people meet because tangible connection outshines high-speed communication.
- The fear of being out of the loop represents a possible fear of being left out.
- If a company is to embrace globalization and 24/7 accessibility, it must create a policy for its practical deployment, including time allocations for answering multi-time-zone phone inquiries.
- "No" is often perceived as a bad word and this fuels our fear of saying no. Those who *slow* down can learn the art of negotiation, which seeks a mutually acceptable mid-ground.
- The fear of emptiness looks at the discomfort some people feel with silence and inactivity. There is a strategic advantage in allowing silence to enter into conversations and meetings. Silence and inactivity are usually key watersheds in the development of creative ideas.

HOW TO *COOL DOWN*

- How has the fear of losing your job (or losing a promotion) influenced your approach to implementing change?
- When you feel fear, what do you do about it?
- Have you ever written your fears out and analyzed them "as an outsider?"
- Remember that written "Fear Statements" can be used as part of a discussion with a manager or customer. Tangible demonstrations of your plans and concerns can go a long way towards identifying a mutually acceptable solution.
- What irks you at work? What small or large sources of friction can you identify? What approach might you take to ensure this friction does not fester? Consider, for example, having a meeting with the person who is the source of the friction, possibly with a third person (a mediator) in the room.
- What fears do you have about your clients? In what ways do you fear offending them? Use the following checklist to help with your answers:
    - In what way do I fear my actions will offend my customer?
    - What is my customer expecting of me?
    - Why does the customer do business with me in the first place?
    - What do I believe will drive the customer away?
    - What can I do to counteract this?
    - Have I recently taken the time to ask all of my customers these questions?
- When you feel conflict or other uncomfortable issues coming along, what is your chosen method of communication? Why? Could you identify a better means to communicate?
- Similarly, when you feel conflict or other uncomfortable issues coming along, what is your tendency to deal with it? Do you take it on right away, or do you procrastinate? Why do you think this is? What might be a better way of resolving this issue?
- When you feel obliged to say "yes" to another person's request, how many other options do you consider before agreeing? For example, could you:

- Negotiate to do the task at a later time?
- Suggest a different person who might be able to take it on?
- Offer to do part of the task instead of all of it?
- Offer to trade one task for another?
- Assist the requestor in locating possible alternate solutions?
- Say yes to the requestor on the condition that she observes, learns, and takes accountability for this task next time?
- Have you ever feared emptiness/silence? Why? What does it represent to you? What might emptiness/silence do *for* you if it were given a chance?

1 Charlie Brown, Lucy, and *A Charlie Brown Christmas* are © United Feature Syndicate Inc.
2 Friedman, Thomas, L. *The World Is Flat: A Brief History of the Twenty-first Century*. Farrar Straus Giroux, Expanded and Updated edition (April 30, 2006), pp. 324-325.
3 http://knowledge.wharton.upenn.edu/index.cfm?fa=viewfeature&id=1398 Feb 27, 2006
4 Ibid.

BUSY AS YOU ARE,

THERE'S NO TIME LIKE THE PRESENT

TO CARVE YOUR FUTURE.

CHAPTER 9

CAREER MAINTENANCE

David Bowie is a rock musician whose longevity is due partly to his chameleon-like ability to reinvent himself every few years. He is also the namesake of the "Bowie Theory," coined by Princeton University economist, Alan Krueger. Bowie, he said, had told the *New York Times* in 2002 that "music itself is going to become like running water or electricity," which was a far-sighted reference to its current ubiquity and accessibility via the Internet. Professor Krueger's theory points out how the increase in concert ticket prices can be directly attributed to the new methods by which consumers can access their favorite tunes. Rather than purchase LPs or CDs from a store as in previous decades, most people are now likely to download, often for free or for a very small fee, just a selected song or two from numerous artists.

With the revenue stream from record sales now substantially diminished, many musicians are recognizing the apparent reversal. Instead of cheap concerts fueling a demand for record sales, the tunes now must fuel a demand for the live show, for a live show experience cannot be reproduced digitally and that is where the big money is now to be found. In other words, the human contact experience has become a matchless commodity. As Bowie said to his fellow performers, "You'd better be prepared for doing a lot of touring, because that's really the only unique situation that's going to be left."[1]

For those of us who are not rock stars, a similar Bowie effect exists. Many components of our professional offerings are being affected by new technologies: Hotel operators have to compete against teleconferencing and web casting; package tour operators must compete against online travel websites. Physicians must deal with patients who arrive armed with a great deal of medical information (and misinformation) gleaned from the Internet. Book retailers must take on Amazon.com and all the great media giants now recognize that consumers can find alternate sources of entertainment wherever and whenever they want. As discussed in Chapter 1, accountants, lawyers, consultants, and other professionals are seeing a growing trend of their "bread and butter" work being transferred offshore. Yet we soldier on, nose to the grindstone, moving from task to task, meeting to meeting, email to email, seldom looking up. Parkinson's Law swoops in to fill every second with busy-ness, leaving no room for the future. We live, time-wise, hand to mouth. The future doesn't have an appointment. The schedule is full.

In Chapter 2, in the case study of Bruno, Karen, Vern, and Lisa, we observed how a full 50 minutes or more could have been made available through the use of clear, direct communication rather than email badminton. Now it's time to consider what could have been done with that block of 50 minutes of lost time. Four separate opportunities spring to mind, all of which do indeed belong to your future.

THE FUTURE OF YOUR CURRENT JOB

What Are You Doing to Network at Work?

What are you doing to consciously and consistently build the anchor points of your future? Are you giving yourself time to *cool down* and connect with the right people inside your company or your industry who can help you:

- Get in touch with the right resources for solving problems quickly
- Find the right answer for a procedure or problem

- Score prime resources for an upcoming project
- Help identify needs and opportunities
- Learn more about what's actually going on, politically and strategically?

This is an example of how knowledge, which becomes power, is available to anyone who consciously chooses to seek it. By making sure you are closely tied to the grapevine rather than just being pressed constantly to the grindstone, you become more politically connected and your chances of thriving increase. Kathleen Reardon, author of *The Secret Handshake*, highlights how much of the information about project success, for example, who the key power-holders are, and how they might impact your own plans, comes from the ability to "read between the lines of politics and conversation."[2] You've already seen this in some simple examples mentioned throughout this book. Consider the importance of:

- Allowing pauses and silence in meetings and in conversations
- Being able to read body language and subtle facial cues
- Active listening
- Managing up
- Managing conversation flow.

A well-maintained network may make the vital difference between staying employed and losing your position. It may be the element that determines whether you stay where you are in an organization or whether you will be able to move up. Those who are too busy to see which way the wind is blowing may not see storm clouds—or favorable breezes approaching—until it is too late.

More subtle, perhaps, but equally important are the personal talents that grow out of such connections. One of Reardon's key strategies for political sophistication as it applies to career management is that of improving your powers of observation. "Listening for informational or emotional content isn't enough," she says, "... effective listening means not just hearing what your boss or peer said ... but determining what he or she *meant* as well ... it's important to be able to tell when you're being sent a message of encouragement."[3]

Have you ever passed up on an opportunity to network or to have lunch because it seems like there's no place in your schedule for it?

What Are You Doing to Spend Time with a Mentor?

What are you doing to ensure you have access to 50 minutes with someone who's "been there and done that" already; someone who can give you the fruit of 20 years or more of his experience? Do you have time in your schedule to find a mentor, schedule time with him, and actually see this person? Richard Branson's mentor was Sir Freddie Laker. Alexander the Great was mentored by Aristotle. No doubt your manager also had someone she turned to for advice and hard-won wisdom. In any area of business—sales, management, strategy, you name it—most successful people not merely had a mentor, they had the presence of mind to seek one out.

There are many types of mentors that can be approached for help:

- **A retired professional.** Such a mentor comes with decades of experience, whether within your own company or elsewhere and is someone who would probably be more than happy to share (or sell) his wisdom.
- **Your manager.** By asking the person to whom you report to be your mentor, you accomplish the dual victory of learning from an experienced guide as well as keeping in close communication with the person who assigns your work. This is an excellent way to renegotiate deadlines and balance priorities.
- **A colleague within the company.** Such a mentor can either provide answers or simply be the receiver while you hear yourself talk.
- **A colleague at another company** (within the bounds of confidentiality, of course).
- **Your company's own mentorship program.** Many organizations have an established mentorship program run through the HR or Employee Assistance Program (EAP) department.
- **An exterior professional coach or mentor.**
- **A volunteer steering committee.** This is essential for self-employed entrepreneurs.

- **Biographies.** A world of mentorship awaits within the pages of biographies. There are thousands of books detailing the lives of all manner of people, famous and infamous, successes and failures, all of which provide mentorship through their experiences. It's a far better use of your lunchtime, in my opinion, to take a walk and listen to a spoken-word biography or to actually read a biography rather than spend lunch working over your keyboard.

What Are You Doing to Become a Mentor?

Equally important to having a mentor is being one. Successful people from all stripes have learned the importance of giving, not just with their checkbook, but with something far more valuable: their time. Some actually refer to the time they give to others as tithing, since it carries the same types of importance and reward as those who tithe to their church. The act of giving is an essential component in the creation of a successful person, not merely in the altruistic sense in terms of what is given to someone else, but also in the personal development of a person as both a human being and a professional.

Every mentoring relationship in which I have been involved as well as those that I have talked about with others has proven to be of mutual benefit. Every mentor learns something about herself at the same time as she shares her wisdom with her student. That is what is so great about mentoring. There's really no sacrifice, just double profit. I've already discussed the value of hearing yourself speak ideas as an exercise in personal proofing (Chapter 7). Cognitive psychologists will tell you that such activities serve as an act of mental programming, which firms up ideas much more strongly than if they stay sloshing about in your short-term memory. When you hear yourself dispense your own advice to a student, you become your own audience. Your own words and thoughts re-enter your mind through your ears and are vetted, assessed, and reinforced.

Can you find 50 minutes a month to be available to others in the business who can learn from you? Altruism aside, these people's lives are as rich with promise and potential as your own. You never know where a mentored individual might end up and what mutual benefits might accrue in the future. Can anyone afford not to *cool down* enough to include at least one mentor in her network?

What Are You Doing to Manage Up?

We saw in Chapter 7 that "managing up" refers to the art of managing your manager. Now there's a scary thought. One of the single greatest disconnects in corporate life is the inability for managers and their people to communicate effectively. When either side is always too busy, misunderstandings can quickly grow into larger, less productive relationships. Managing up is not about being confrontational, of course. It's about informing your manager of your state of busy-ness and the projects you are working on; it's about heading off surprises or crises before they happen.

Tips on How to Manage Your Manager

- Know what time orientation your manager has: Is he more receptive in the morning or in the afternoon?
- When are his busier times? His quieter times? During which do you think he would prefer to be approached?
- Is he a scheduler or an *ad hoc* type of person? Would he react better to a scheduled meeting or is it better to "pounce" on him?
- Is he a control freak? An egotist? How does he prefer to communicate with you? What do you know about his openness to discussion?
- What kind of personality is he? Type A or B?
- How much time do you think you should allow for a meeting?
- How will you prepare the agenda?
- Can you clearly identify your objectives?
- Remember that not only might you need to schedule this meeting, the onus might be on you to maintain the follow-through: to schedule the next meeting or to ensure that the next items happen as they should.
- Take responsibility for ensuring that clear communication is given the time and attention it requires.

Managing up is not unidirectional. Many times the onus may be on you to find out what your manager is up to, for instance, what travel plans she has made, what projects she is working on. Of course this takes tact and discretion, but overall, those who are able to manage up get more from their day and their career than those who keep their heads down.

Firefighting

Often I will be called in to a company to work with employees who say that fighting fires is a central component of their work. Not literal fires, of course, but crises: unexpected problems and short-term, urgent issues, usually involving a customer or a supplier. Though these staff members consider firefighting to be fundamental to their job, they also admit that it is a prime source of stress.

The solution comes not from learning how to fight fires more quickly, but from careful planning and communication with the appropriate stakeholders. Since firefighting is perceived to be about dealing reactively to a situation that is unfolding right now, the challenge I set to people is to anticipate and ideally prepare for fires before they happen. That way, the crisis tasks become part of the norm, rather than an unwelcome intrusion into an overloaded schedule. The key to crisis preparation is threefold:

- Make time in your schedule to review the nature and frequency of past crises: Where did they happen? When? How? What caused them? How long did it take to resolve the crisis? How many people did it take? What was the opinion of those involved (clients, those affected within the company) to your reaction to the situation? Most important, what are the odds of the same crisis happening again? Next time, what will you do differently?

    Notice that I suggested you *make time* for this. That's because such review is easy to overlook when days get busy. But this is why the closure is so important. Closure is about ending a project or crisis and reviewing it, so you can learn from it.

- Allow enough time in your schedule to plan your future days and weeks, and include time for possible crises based on your knowledge of them to date. If the crisis doesn't hit, there will always be more work that can fill the space, but if it does hit, both your schedule and your mind will be better able to handle them.
- Manage your manager to ensure all of you are on the same page about the present, the future, and all the possibilities that these may hold. This rule doesn't simply apply across and downwards to the people you work with and who report to you. It also means upwards, to the person who is ultimately in charge of your job.

That is the challenge that I set for my clients, and it is the same one I ask of you:

- Do you have time in your day to slow down and connect with your boss to make sure the two of you are on the same page?
- Do you have time in your day to think clearly about all of the tasks and crises that make up your workload?
- Do you have time in your day to think clearly enough to plan the next meeting and to influence the manager to be there?

As Stanley Bing writes in his excellent book *Throwing the Elephant*, the onus may very well be upon you to influence the boss's actions, to schedule this "managing-up meeting," and to create its agenda.[4] You will have to decide when and how the meeting will be held, taking into consideration your manager's schedule and personality type. For example, some managers are attracted to regularly scheduled meetings, maybe at 8:00 a.m. every second Monday. Others may be less attracted to that type of structure, but will react well to a quick chat in the kitchenette or in the elevator. It may be up to you to schedule and strategize these meetings, to feed your manager the information you need to impart, and to extract from her the information you need to have. As Bing suggests, it's up to you to look after your manager in the interest of proactive time management and to avoid future fires.

Strategic Managing Up

Managing up is not just about dealing with immediate crises, either. Those who spend their entire day with their nose to the grindstone are not necessarily the ones who will advance as far as they could. Part of the success that comes when managing up is combined with *cooling down* comes from being shrewd enough to see what and who is out there, and then to strategically make your presence known. Kathleen Reardon puts it this way:

> Being dedicated doesn't necessarily mean putting in long hours or being constantly available. To the contrary, it's important to put in long hours and be available when it matters to those in a position to notice your extra dedication. Otherwise you're headed for burnout, and your extra effort just becomes expected rather than the important contribution it really is.[5]

Time spent in a strategic huddle with one's manager is an opportunity for self-promotion as much as it is for dealing with immediacies. This goes back to the concept of selling, in Chapter 7. What does your manager know about your current achievements? Your aspirations? Your ideas for innovation? You may have told him a year or more ago, but a year is a long time. It's up to you to set up such a meeting, to schedule the agenda, and to identify the objectives.

Remember also to put yourself in your customer's shoes—your customer in this case being your manager. Is the act of scheduling a strategic managing-up meeting with him really an unwelcome intrusion? Or might he see it as proof of your potential for more responsible assignments? By contrast, if you were to choose not to "bother" him in this way, would that leave him in peace, or would it demonstrate a lack of initiative on your part? Here again is the value inherent in *cooling down*: It's not just about the time required to have a meeting—it's also about the strategic assessment of the implications of having or not having such a meeting. Going through this process will have a great impact on your future.

Implementation

These four concepts—internal networking, having a mentor, being a mentor, and managing up—all require time and acceptance of the value of *cooling down*. I try to ask people to think about the tithing example once again. Traditional tithing, in the religious context requested that 10 percent of a person's income be given over to their church. Could you assign 10 percent of your workweek to these types of activities? Probably not, because your calendar at this moment is likely already full. So let's quantify your workload a little, just like a project manager would: How many hours on average do you put in at the office, not counting work that you take home (which you shouldn't do anyway)? This number of hours might be available to you if you have been practicing the strategies in the "How to *Cool Down*" segments at the end of each chapter, specifically, in this case, Chapter 1. The higher the number of hours you admit to working, the more you need to put 10 percent away for mentoring, networking, and managing up. If you work a 40- to 45-hour week, then you should spend four hours, or 50 minutes a day on maintaining your career.

Too busy to contemplate that? Perhaps the lunch hour could be your salvation. Keith Ferrazzi is a great proponent of lunchtime networking. In his book, *Never Eat Alone*, he demonstrates just how valuable it is to allow the time to identify and connect with people, not just any people, even though everyone we meet has connections to other people, but, specifically to what he calls "super-connectors," those people who are hubs in the network of survival:

> ... what's most important is developing deep and trusting relationships, not superficial contacts. ... I believe friendships are the foundation for a truly powerful network. For most of us, cultivating a lengthy list of mere acquaintances on top of the effort devoted to your circle of friends is just too draining. The thought of being obligated to another hundred or so people—sending birthday cards, dinner invites, and all that stuff that we do for those close to us—seems outlandishly taxing.

Only, for some, it's not. These people are super-connectors. People like me who maintain contact with thousands of people. The key, however, is not only that we know thousands of people but that we know thousands of people in many different worlds, and we know them well enough to give them a call. Once you become friendly with a super-connector, you're only two degrees away from the thousands of different people we know.[6]

Your 50 minutes of career management could unfold like this:

- Reserve 40 out of those 50 minutes a day for the actual lunch, whether you eat with a colleague/mentor/friend or enjoy a biography as mentioned earlier. And lunch, by the way, need not be in an expensive restaurant. Great conversations can happen equally easily over sandwiches.

- Reserve the other 10 minutes out of those 50 minutes a day to contact someone, whether to invite them to meet you for lunch, or simply to drop them a line, asking how they are doing. No sales, no pressure, just a simple, genuine inquiry as to how they are. There's no need for them to call back, if they don't wish to. It's enough that you just remind them you're around. This is network maintenance, and it inoculates your livelihood against rot and atrophy by rebuilding your fading image in the minds of people whom you've met. If you can do this almost daily, each weekday of the year, you will be able to keep up to 240 people (as well as all of the people they know) aware of your presence and potential.

THE FUTURE OF YOUR CAREER

Careers are dynamic. The progress of a career is seldom linear and predictable. Careers have a life of their own, just like companies do. It's hard to picture companies as mortal, but they are. They eventually die, or they get eaten (bought up) by someone else. The average life expectancy of a multinational Fortune 500 company is now between 40 and 50 years. "A full one-third of the companies listed in the 1970

Fortune 500, for instance, had vanished by 1983—acquired, merged, or broken to pieces. Human beings have learned to survive, on average, for 75 years or more, but there are very few companies that are that old and flourishing."[7]

With such instability comes an absolute need to pave your own path and to hunt down your own destiny, whether your preferred stomping grounds are within the walls of your current organization, or out there, in the wilds of commerce or entrepreneurship. And this applies whether you consider yourself to be a go-getter entrepreneurial type, or a quieter craftsperson. There comes a time in many a professional's life when she recognizes the true value of networking, and that is usually the day just after she has been let go, or downsized, or depending on how you look at it, "rightsized" from her employer. I have worked with many people in this situation over the years and have observed and empathized with them as they sat, shell-shocked and paralyzed, suddenly seeing themselves as a PWI: a person without identity. In North America, as with much of the business-oriented world, we define ourselves by our work. It's very difficult to maintain the flow of a conversation in a social situation without quickly coming to the phrase, "So what do you do?"

The moment the axe falls, unless a person is well prepared, shock and stress override everything, and depression is quick to follow. To have met this person just a month or so before he was aware of his fate, he would most likely have appeared very busy—too busy with the work of the day to entertain the notion of networking events or mentorship. He was probably grabbing a quick sandwich over the keyboard but had no time for anything purely social.

Once again the speed of the present distorts clear vision into the future. Strategy is overruled by the immediate. It's difficult, when a person's mind is busy processing three, four, or five simultaneous urgencies, to reflect on the strategic value of networking, since its value cannot always be quantified on some intellectual balance sheet. Its payoff might occur somewhere in the months and years to come in ways not immediately imaginable or predictable. When faced with another high-speed day, a networking event is a sheer impossibility: Seen through the tunnel vision of the daily To-Do List it appears as a frivolous waste of an hour—an hour that (it seems) could be better spent clearing off an extra task or two. And that's where the problem starts to fester. In the trapeze act that is your career, your personal network represents one of the two ropes that hold up the bar on which you swing. When paired with the other rope, representing your talents and experience, you have the tools to keep moving. But if one should fail, the show is over.

In Person: The Value of Slowing Down and Networking

There are many great books out there that teach great things about networking—why it is important and how to do it—so I will restrict my comments to talking specifically about how *cool* beats fast in this vital area of career management. Quite simply, speed networking doesn't work terribly well. When busy people find themselves at an event such as a Chamber of Commerce meeting where networking is the primary reason for being there, or at an association lunch event where networking is the unspoken reason for being there, they can easily become overwhelmed at the prospect of choosing which people to connect with, how many is the right number, and whether it is of any use at all. An easy rule of thumb is three. Three new people. Any more than that and networking becomes too hard to manage. But it is easy to move to three different conversations during a one-hour event or during the breaks of longer functions. Just set yourself a time limit, of perhaps 10 minutes for each conversation, and then move on. The magic number three has been used for thousands of years as the truly functional collection of people, and it applies to meeting new people too. Aim for three. It makes the challenge of meeting new people less onerous, and you will remember each of them better.

Remembering Names

This is a fundamental rule of positive networking, but very often a person's name can go skipping out of our memory because it's new to us. This leaves people in an awkward or at least less-impressive situation at the close of the conversation. The secret to easily remembering names is in word association: Creatively connect a person's physical resemblance or a feature of their appearance such as clothing or hairstyle to a word or person from your past. There's no real magic to it; it just takes a prepared, *cool* mind. If a person's name starts with F, such as Francis, and she wears glasses, you might be able to associate *F*rances with *F*rames. A bald-headed man called Mike might remind you of a microphone. A person with black hair whose name is Cameron might remind you of the black case of a camera. Anyone can train themselves to remember three names, at least, during a social situation, but the mind must be open to and primed for the opportunity by not being overrun by thoughts and speed during the social function. When the opportunity presents itself, you must slow down just enough to silently and discreetly commit this name to memory by way of this word-association technique. The speed of reaction that is the hallmark of a social introduction must be replaced by *slow*. In return you will be able to add polish to the relationship, concluding it with the most impressive, memorable, and noteworthy words in the English language: the name of the person to whom you are speaking.

Just for a moment, pretend your name is Pat. Think to yourself which of the following two closures would make a greater impression on you:

- "It was really nice to meet you. We should talk again soon."
- "Pat, it was really nice to meet you. We should talk again soon."

Most people will be far more impressed by the second one and will be more likely to stay warm to the possibility of further involvement with you.

Know How You Look

This topic is covered in depth in Chapter 7, so there's no need to repeat it here. In short, best impressions are made when you not only look the way you want, but when you *know* you look the way you want. Grooming and personal presentation are of paramount importance in establishing and furthering business relationships. Yet people who rush seldom get the chance to make sure they look as good as they can. Slight imperfections such as a misaligned tie or windblown hair may seem minor, while more serious imperfections such as a stain or food between the teeth can be outright embarrassing. The main point, though, is that the memory of the imperfection will last in the minds of those you meet.

Listen Actively

A further benefit of slowing down is realized through the practiced art of delivering social satisfaction, that is, in demonstrating active listening. This concept was touched upon in Chapter 7. Active listening requires more than just appropriately timed head nods. It refers, first and foremost, to allowing your conversation partner to do most of the talking and then demonstrating you have heard and that you care about what she is saying by repeating the key facts and inserting positive commentary or questions as appropriate. Whether these social situations occur inside or outside of the work environment, every person with whom you interact will be affected by your actions and image.

Give Business Cards "Face"

Regardless of where your social interactions take place, whether inside or outside the work environment, every person you relate to is affected by your actions and image. When it comes to meeting new people, even their business card needs to be "listened to." When handed a business card, expert networkers don't simply glance at it quickly and then pocket it. No. They use the power of *slow*. They receive the card and give it a good look-over, examining its design, the address information, and the person's name and professional designations. To use a phrase from Eastern culture, this is called giving "face."

Such prolonged attention to a small piece of cardstock? It may seem strange to the uninitiated and certainly seems to have no place in a time-pressed business world. However, when giving a card *face*, you're not really giving your prolonged attention to the card; you're giving attention to the person whom the card represents. Face is a gift of legitimacy. It recognizes the hard work and effort the owner of the card is putting into her career, and it telegraphs to her that, yes, you care about her effort. That's what the card-reading activity does, and that's why active listening is so important and so profitable. People need to feel they are important and to know they are important—two different concepts. They need to receive the message that the time they spend in the company of another person is valued and that they are being taken seriously.

Close Memorably

The old expression "you never get a second chance to make a first impression" may be true, but there is an addendum to that rule: You always get a chance to make a last impression. In psychology there is a concept called the mental "law of primacy," which states that when given a line of faces or a list of objects, most people remember the first face or object more vividly than the rest. But this law is complemented by the "law of recency," which states that people are also very good at remembering the last in a list of items. Both are possible simultaneously within the same person, which means that the faces or items in the middle of a line or group tend to fade the fastest. This is important to remember when choosing your place in a receiving line at a corporate function. Aim for the beginning or the end, never the middle, if you want to be remembered. It's also why receptionists are (or should be) counted among the most important people in any organization. The receptionist is the first person a visitor encounters (primacy), and she is also the last person a visitor deals with upon leaving (recency). The receptionist's greeting and tone of voice, her "thank-you," and overall demeanor leave a mark that will be remembered as part of the overall emotional impression of a company or organization.

In the business of networking and career management, this is yet another avenue where the power of *slow* pays off big time. Consider the following items; together they form a closing sequence that ensures ongoing benefit to the person who slows down enough to use them:

- *Maintaining eye contact during the closing conversation.* Are you able to transfer your mental state during this face-to-face interaction from *reactive* to *proactive*? Are you able to consciously maintain clear eye contact? To deliver genuine warmth, interest, and respect from your eyes to those of the person you're talking to?

- *Making full use of the other person's name.* This is described in more detail above, as in "Pat, it was a genuine pleasure to meet you."
- *Following through.* After the conversation has ended and the person has moved away, take the time, *before doing anything else,* to discreetly note all the important information about that person, especially reminders regarding any follow-up activities that were promised. I prefer to do this on the back of their business card in preparation for the next step, below.
- *Ensuring time to actually enter the reminders and follow-ups into your calendar system.* These reminders may refer to actual documents or information to be sent; they may also refer to "ticklers," as in, when you should next touch base with this person. Is she a once-every-three-months contact or a once-a-year contact? Based on the 50-minute principle of networking described earlier, are you going to be able to slow down enough to keep in touch with this person, before your memories of each other fade away? It's a great shame, the number of people who get forgotten during a professional's lifetime. All people have a limited memory for faces and names, and most will forget a new person within six months if not reminded. One of the benefits of working a little slower is that time is made available to contact at least one person in your network each day; you can let them hear your voice, simply be reminded of your existence, and therefore keep the relationship warm.
- *Sending a thank-you note.* If this person warrants a thank-you note, will you have the time to send one? Will you have the time to remember why it's important to send one? As corny as it may sound, there are few things more effective in terms of getting ahead than a handwritten thank-you note. One reason: they take time to write. Another reason: they're personal. Just a simple hand-written note, on a blank card. People often ask me why thank-you notes can't be sent by email, which is, after all, much quicker. But the answer lies within that very question. To take the time to thank someone with a handwritten card demonstrates to the recipient that you are using your most precious commodity—time—to express in a very human way the value of the relationship or of the time spent

together. Not everyone, of course, has a calligraphist's talent for ornate penmanship, but that doesn't matter. Provided the time is taken to hand-write clearly and legibly, the message will get through positively and memorably.

So there. We have just described five powerful ways of making an impact on people in any social situation. These activities are all dividends that come from slowing down enough to be a) aware of and b) capable of exploiting the positive elements of human interaction. People need to feel they are important. They need to receive the message that they are valued and that they are being taken seriously. They will open the door to your next opportunity, whether they themselves become a buyer of your services, a supplier of wisdom, or a conveyer of your positive reputation to others.

The reasons for these techniques—remembering, listening, closing, and following up—is not to be nice for the sake of being nice, but to market, to develop, and to leverage your personal brand in order to build an insurance policy for career furtherance or career salvation. Jobs don't last. Companies don't last. But mortgages, payments, and bills do. If you're too busy right now to *cool down* and touch base with someone, keeping their name alive in your system and your name alive in theirs, then you really do risk erasing part of your own future.

LIFELONG LEARNING LEADS TO LIFELONG EMPLOYABILITY

It is extremely rare for a company to be able to guarantee job security, and why should they when the nature of business, of work, and of consumer demands change so fast? And when the marketplace changes so fast, it only makes sense that we, as active participants in it, do the same.

There was also a time when higher education meant investing three or four years or more of full-time study at a college or university before starting a career. Thankfully, there are now other options. Lifelong learning offered through online classes means that anyone with access to a computer and the Internet can further his academic and vocational skills, and consequently his professional destiny, one course at a time.

This is yet another demonstration of how the benefits of the *slow* movement can pay off.

Studying on Company Time

One of the projects my company has undertaken and continued with over the years has to do with getting permission for staff members to take courses during company time. All the Internet access in the world won't help if the prevailing attitude from management is "Don't let it interfere with your duties." I've worked with nurses, advertising people, accountants, and assistants, all of whom say, "I can't focus on my studies when I'm being called away all the time."

So I stand firm on the following three points:

- People do their best studying during the day.
- The future of many a professional's career and the future of the company that employs her, both rest on the employee's ability to upgrade her skills and knowledge on a regular basis.
- Employee retention is not based on financial incentives alone. Job satisfaction, the opportunity to further oneself, and acknowledgement from superiors all play major roles in deciding whether to stay with an employer or to move on.

How many hours per week are required for an employee to take a course? I suggest three hours a week of focused reading time or online lab time. Is it possible for three hours to be squeezed out of a busy 40- or 50-hour workweek? The answer is "yes," based on the principles of Parkinson's Law outlined in Chapter 1. The very nature of humans at work means that distractions, false urgencies, and the general sense of busy-ness already described tend to fill the time available. Finally, three hours can successfully be found and carved out of a workweek, if both the employee and her manager can agree that:

- Time spent studying on company time does not waste company time: It is an investment in developing the company's internal talents and abilities as well as those of a loyal employee.

- Employees who are given undisturbed time to study (perhaps one hour at a time) will emerge from their studies refreshed and energetic. Even though the course material might be challenging, by virtue of being different from the regular workload, it still amounts to a change in routine, which energizes and refocuses the brain.
- The time for studying can be found, if together you look hard enough.

This last point integrates the principles of *slow* described throughout this book. If the employee were to try by herself to find the time to study, she would be beset with interruptions, resistance, and guilt. But *together*, as manager and employee, schedules and tasks can be reviewed, and permission can be granted. Twenty emails that up until now might have taken an hour to respond to, might just as easily and completely be dealt with in half-an-hour, when the motivation and permission are in place.

That's the type of thing that *slow* can do. It finds space where there seemingly was none before. How? Not by working faster, but by taking the time to think, communicate, plan, and refine. By perceiving and then avoiding the pull of Parkinson's Law, you can ensure time is put aside for study during the day—on company time where it belongs.

THE FUTURE OF YOUR PAST: WHAT DID I DO?

Let me tell you another story. As part of my own mentoring involvement, I had lunch with a young law student. She was preparing to graduate and wished to develop her good work habits early as an inoculation against the heavy workloads she knew would be facing her as a junior lawyer. True to my views on the mutual benefits derived from mentoring, during lunch she told *me* a wonderful story. She had just dined recently with a prominent criminal lawyer, someone well known on the national legal stage as a figurehead who fought precedent-setting cases in which plenty of media exposure was assured. He was nearing 65 and was successful both professionally and financially. When the young student asked him for advice, however, he simply said, "I can teach you nothing." When she asked him to elaborate, he admitted that although his practice was a success, it had come at the cost of not knowing his family, his children, and grandchildren; of missing ball games, recitals, graduations, even anniversaries because of his consistently heavy case load and a desire to work all-out, all the time. Though he had enjoyed a great legal career, he had not had a life.

This story reminded me of a similar tale told by Steven Covey, in his book, *First Things First*, in which he describes a successful business executive who builds a multigenerational home to house his kids and his grandkids in a desperate attempt to buy back the family time he had used up while preoccupied with building his business.[8] I know of many other parents, too many, who, out of fear of not putting in enough face time, or due to the myth that busy-ness equals business, lose contact with their kids and their other loved ones.

One of the worst casualties of a high-speed life is the tunnel vision it generates. It is easy to justify staying late to get caught up or to empty the in-box. It may even seem like there is no other choice. But after 20 or 30 years, even the wealthiest magnate realizes there is one thing that can never be bought back, and that, of course, is time. Choosing to adopt *cool* principles is a life decision. As you seek to figure out whether you are willing to do this, I would ask you to consider the following question: Is the personal price you're paying for your success really worth it? In other words, what is the cost of your money?

You have true power over your career. Take some time and assess its pros and the cons. Write these things down. Above all, don't let it get lost in the blur.

KEY POINTS TO TAKE AWAY

- The *Bowie Theory* identified that music is going to become ubiquitous like running water or electricity, which points to the fact that the human element, live concerts in the case of music, will make the difference in the future.
- Networking internally means taking the time to hook up with contacts that can save you time and keep you in touch.
- Mentors are an essential component of career furtherance.
- Being a mentor allows for simultaneous teaching and learning.
- Managing up is about solidifying a relationship of communication and understanding between you and your manager. The onus may be upon you to start this and to maintain it as a regular habit.
- Careers are dynamic. As such, it's prudent to invest time in preparing for your next few years in case the axe falls sometime soon.
- Networking is best done through active listening, giving "face" to business cards, and actively following up.
- Memorable closes are essential because they leverage the psychological law of recency.
- Lifelong learning is an essential part of every professional's career and should be pursued during productive workday hours rather than late at night.
- We can learn from those who have gone before us and have become successful at the cost of their personal or family life.
- Use some *slow* time to ensure access to lifelong learning, and therefore lifelong employability.
- *Slow* isn't just about the quality of work. It's also about the quality of your life, health, and experience.

HOW TO *COOL DOWN*

- Make a wish list. What do you see yourself doing in five years? 10? 20?
- What activities do you want your working life to entail?
- How about your non-working life (home, friends, family)?
- Could you use this written wish list when next talking to your manager about your career path or annual review?
- How strong is your current network? How often do you contact people just to network?
- Have you identified the "important" people in your contact list?
- Respecting the bounds of your current employers' confidentiality, are you able to keep a separate list of the key people and contacts you have met and who may be personally valuable to you over the years? Are you able to keep that list offsite?
- Does every "important" person in this list have a "tickler"? That is to say, a reminder to keep in touch? Not everyone should be contacted every week, of course. Some people could do with a call every six months or so, others perhaps once a year.
- Have you ever had a conversation with a manager or mentor in which the discussion seemed to be "deeper" than just immediate projects? How would you react to and follow up on possible "between-the-lines" messages? What mentors do you have lined up who could coach you in this vital skill?
- What mentors do you have in general? How do you (or might you) schedule time once a week to talk with one of them?
- Who can you be a mentor to? How might you go about publicizing this? What benefits would you expect from a mentoring relationship?
- How much time can you *make* in your week or month to manage up? What kind of manager do you work for? How best might she be approached e.g., scheduled meeting or *ad hoc*?
- Who can you have lunch with this week?
- What formal networking events willl you attend this month?

• What plans do you have for additional learning, e.g., college courses of professional vocational courses? What would be the best time of day for you to study? How will you approach your manager with your plan for lifelong learning?

1 Pareles, Jon. 2002. "David Bowie, 21st-Century Entrepreneur." *The New York Times* (June 9): 30., quoted in Krueger, Alan B., *The Economics of Real Superstars: The Market for Rock Concerts in the Material World*, Princeton University (April 2004) http://www.irs.princeton.edu/pubs/pdfs/484.pdf

2 Reardon, Kathleen Kelley, PhD., *The Secret Handshake: Mastering the Politics of the Business Inner Circle*. Currency Books, 2001, pp. 87-88.

3 Ibid.

4 Bing, Stanley, *Throwing the Elephant: Zen and the Art of Managing Up*. Collins, 2003.

5 Reardon, p. 88.

6 Ferrazzi, Keith, *Never Eat Alone, and Other Secrets to Success, One Relationship at a Time*. Currency (February 22, 2005).

7 De Geus, Airie, *The Living Company: Habits for Survival in a Turbulent Business Environment*. Harvard Business School Press; 1st edition (June 4, 2002).

8 Covey, Steven, Merrill, Roger, and Merrill, Rebecca, *First Things First: To Live, to Love, to Learn, to Leave a Legacy*. Free Press, 1996.

THE LOSS OF MY JOB,

THE LOSS OF ALL THAT I AM?

A NEW DOOR OPENS.

CHAPTER 10

TRANSITION

The dreaded period called *transition,* a nice term for unemployment, is a situation that people think is the last place in the world where a *cool, slow* approach would be appropriate. When you are unemployed, the busyness of work comes to a screeching stop and all of a sudden Monday is no longer the beginning of another week in the rat race. Instead, it represents the start of five long days of emptiness and despair.

Even if you yourself are currently employed as you read these words, and you feel you are too busy to think about anything other than your overloaded schedule, it is still worthwhile to read this chapter for two important reasons:

1. The skills and techniques described here aren't just for those who happen to find themselves out of work. They reinforce the idea that above all, the best thing you can possibly do to improve your ability to sell, to influence, to be productive, to remain employable, and to get things done is to *cool down.*

2. You might not be employed in your current job this time next year (or even next month). No-one's job is very secure anymore. In

that case, learning now about these strategies will cut out a lot of stress and lost time from your own transition period if, or when, it happens.

SHELLSHOCK

When I work with people who have been recently let go, they are often still in shock. Their eyes are glazed, and they have that air of disbelief about them that says, "This can't be happening to me. I'm too good." But it does happen, and it happens to all kinds of good people, especially the hardest-working good people. Often it happens more than once in their lives.

There are two reflexes that often emerge simultaneously alongside the shock of being fired: The first is the desire to protect oneself, and the second is the desire to change the situation—to put things back to rights as quickly as possible. Most recently downsized people feel a desire for fast action; at this juncture, they look to find the first job or offer they can—anything to make up for the fear and indignity of being kicked out of the world of the comfortably employed. This, of course, is a dangerous reaction, since the first offer is seldom the best, and worse, the mental state of a person in shock is not the right one for making career choices.

Consequently, the first thing a person in transition needs to do, quite literally, is to *cool down*—to eliminate the feeling of mounting panic and replace it with a strategy that includes more than simply printing up a résumé and surfing the job sites on the Internet. Many ask me what is the first thing they should do; I usually suggest they go build something.

BUILD A GAZEBO

It was during a workshop, in which I was talking with a group of professionals-in-transition that one gentleman in the audience asked me if it was okay for him to take a week or two and work on building a gazebo in his back yard. It was something he had wanted to do for his family for a long time, but he had never been able to get around to it because he had spent too many weekends stuck at the office. He wanted to know if it was wrong to take time to do this when a part of him felt he really should be out looking for his next job. Clearly, he was looking for permission to step away from the work of finding work. I told him that it was absolutely the right thing to do; in fact, I have long held the belief that everyone in a position of stress, confusion, or overload should go out and build a "gazebo" of his own. Everyone who is thrown into the soul-wrenching position of losing his identity, career, and financial stability should, as a first step, take on some activity that allows him to flush out the panic by using physical distraction, which acts as a catalyst for reflection.

To set out to build a gazebo is to undertake a physical activity in which body and mind become focused on a plan of action that is unrelated to life and its current problems. When both body and mind become occupied in this manner, even when the gazebo-building work gets strenuous, there is relaxation (remember, it's called *eustress*). And when the body and mind relax, blood pressure drops and reflection happens, and then creativity happens.

Some might turn to a week of playing tennis, or of long walks with the dog, or of painting (either with an easel, or on the living room walls with a roller), or of tidying the yard or building a deck. What is most important is that you choose a solitary activity in which body and mind focus on constructive work. There will be time for discussing your findings and thoughts with your partner or mentor later. That's when the holographic brain concept discussed in Chapter 7 will truly shine, the time when you will find yourself answering your own questions. But to begin you need some time to slow down and let the thoughts come.

Remember, this is not a chronic assignment, just as unemployment will not be a chronic condition. The gazebo project might take a week, or two; it symbolizes not just a mind-and-body focused activity but a finite activity as well. Upon completion of the project, you'll be ready for the next chapter of your life.

Slowing down in this fashion allows for significant, salient thoughts to emerge and rise to the top, unfettered by the trivial priorities of email and meetings. Questions such as:

- What do I value?
- What does my next job look like?
- What hours and conditions would suit me best?
- What do I wish to achieve?
- What companies interest me, regardless of whether they currently have openings or not? (We'll cover that later.)

Focusing your mind on an unrelated topic, such as building a gazebo, gives it permission to massage and flex these underlying questions without the stress of hard focus upon them. This is indirect thinking, and in just the same manner that *slow* is quicker than fast when seeking to attain a goal, so indirect thinking leads to resolution faster than direct thinking does.

Here are two perfect examples taken from life chapters of two real people:

- Bob had spent 20 years in the food and beverage industry, soft-drink division, dealing with the logistics of shipping his company's products to regional stores. Not a very exciting statement, is it? While taking some time to paint his house after having been downsized, Bob mulled over the different phrases he could use to describe his qualifications in networking situations. "Food and beverage?" "Shipping?" "Logistics?" All slightly dull until his newly liberated mind hit upon a fact that had been plainly invisible to him for so many years: He worked in the soft-drink industry, one of the world's most popular substances. He suddenly realized that he had something interesting to say; something that would make people remember him. In subsequent networking events he would introduce himself as the person who knew the secret technique that makes Coca-Cola unique. "I can tell you," he would say with a wink, "but then I'd have to kill you." That was something that started conversations. He never gave out the secret, of course, but he was remembered for his novel and intriguing presentation.
- Jane had always been a busy executive and when she was let go, it was her eagerness to get back in the game quickly that proved to be a liability. She wanted to be seen, to have interviews as soon as possible, first thing in the morning. But the people that

she hoped to see at that time were all too busy. They were all in meetings or doing something else. So she forced herself to take some time to walk around the duck pond at the park near her house. Every day. She would ask herself questions, such as, "As a busy executive, if someone were to ask *me* for an appointment, what would be the best time of the day for *me*?" She let this settle in her mind for a while, and soon she hit upon the perfect time when busy professionals, in her experience, are at their most receptive and available: just after coffee break, mid-morning. This became her offering point as she started crafting her pitch. "Let me come and see you at 10:30. I'll spring for coffee," she would say. And that's what she did. She returned to work within the month—just by taking her brain out for a walk around a duck pond.

Tips for Getting Back to Work Quickly

- Establish a work habit that is comfortable to you, e.g., continuing to dress in business clothes while researching and preparing, and setting aside a specific area of the house as your office.
- Set up a second phone line or use your cellphone as the sole contact number. Make sure the line has voice mail.
- Use your email-based network of friends and colleagues to get the word out that you're looking.
- Put bitterness and thoughts of unjust treatment aside. Keep moving forward.
- Remember that luck favors the well prepared.
- Avoid inertia and lethargy during the day. Keep occupied on worthwhile tasks.
- However, avoid also turning the work of finding work into an 18-hour-a-day effort. Keep your evenings and weekends for yourself and your family.
- Make a point of lunching/networking with people who have also been through transition and are now employed again. Learn what worked for them.

I HAVE NO RIGHT TO WORK OUT

Exercise, too, delivers these same intellectual benefits. It's another example of positive stress (*eustress*) influencing the body and delivering oxygen-rich blood to the brain. It's blue-skying just when you need it the most. Yet I have encountered numerous people who see exercise as a privilege of employed people only. That's ironic, really, given that most employed people seldom have the time to exercise on a regular basis. People who are unemployed feel that any time they spend away from the active search for new employment is wasteful self-indulgence. Of course, nothing could be further from the truth. Countless studies have shown that in addition to blood pressure and cardiovascular benefits, exercise does much to elevate mood, to rebalance emotions, and to generate an aura of vibrancy and optimism that can't help but rub off on other people. It's an essential part of your overall job-hunting kit, along with your résumé, your interview skills, your active listening skills, and your visual grooming and presentation.

Remember the principles behind image and first impressions described in Chapter 7? How the emotional side of the brain delivers its signals faster than the rational side? Whether right or wrong, people can't help but make judgments about your appearance, judgments that force their way into an overall assessment. Consider, then, what exercise can do in addition to the cardiovascular and blue-skying opportunities mentioned earlier:

- Your eyes will be brighter and will look less tired and stressed.
- Your posture will be better. Physical exercise helps tone all types of muscles, not just biceps and quads. People who are fit stand straighter and hold their head higher.
- Your clothes will fit better. Improved tone in skin and muscle will make your business clothes look like they were tailor-made.
- Improved breathing ability will help pace conversation flow and deepen vocal tone.
- Exercise also helps bring on top-quality sleep, which ensures top performance the next day.

HOW LONG WILL I BE UNEMPLOYED?

Here's a hard pill to swallow: Many career transition and human resource experts will say that an unemployed professional can expect to be out of work one month for every $10,000 they earn, or expect to earn annually. That means that someone with a $120,000 a year job can reasonably expect to spend a year looking for her next position. This fact may come as a shock to those who have never heard it before and a double-shock to someone already coping with unemployment. But after the initial jolt wears off, this knowledge helps clear away some of the fog caused by confusion and anxiety, and then actually helps set a pace and a style of job hunting that is more appropriate. Once you know it takes time to land a job that fits, it becomes easier to slow down and do it properly.

People who accept the first job offer that comes their way after having been terminated may strike it lucky with a perfect position, sure, but I would bet that has more to do with a well-nurtured network than pure chance. The trouble with accepting the first job that comes along is that it's usually a poor fit, and it makes a person unavailable for the right job, which eventually will come along either through network connections or invention.

For people who still have a job, being aware of this one-month-per-$10,000 ratio helps give greater incentive to *cool down* and invest some time in their future. For, on the one hand, a well-prepared network of contacts and mentors might shorten the time spent in transition. On the other, this knowledge might provide an incentive to prepare financially for a more comfortable transition period. A year of unemployment can be a wonderful thing if money worries do not intervene; it then becomes more like a sabbatical. Those who are too busy to think about the prospects of unemployment may not be able to adjust their spending and saving habits so as to be better prepared for this type of event.

AVOIDING LETHARGY AND DEPRESSION

A key negative development for people not used to looking for work is the sudden cessation of the rat race. Just last week the schedule was full, probably overloaded. There were meetings, deadlines, and activity. Now there is nothing. This change is hard to take for many and can lead to a dangerous spiral of lethargy and depression. Fortunately, there is a solution, and it's the same one that I've been suggesting for all of the other areas of life that this book covers: You must *cool down* enough to see how best to get where you want to go.

In terms of transition, *cooling down* means avoiding these two extremes:

- It means avoiding racing out into the employment marketplace, résumé in hand, ready to accept the first offer that comes along; this smells of desperation.
- It means avoiding burrowing into the sofa, turning on the TV, and coming to a dead stop.

The better route, the saner route, requires that you think through the situation and create a plan, a plan that generates vision, releases energy, and helps you get back on your feet. A transition plan uses the project management principle of thorough planning to recognize that far from there being nothing to do, there is actually a lot to do. You will be as busy during the transition period as you were, and soon will be, back at the office. The types of tasks that need to be done during transition include:

- Drafting a résumé
- Proofing and finalizing the résumé
- Researching companies to target
- Researching their competitors
- Drafting a custom pitch letter
- Proofing the custom pitch letter
- Contacting people in your network
- Scheduling lunches with key contacts
- Attending lunches with key contacts
- Following up after lunches with key contacts
- Identifying networking opportunities
- Attending networking opportunities
- Following up after networking opportunities

- Attending meetings with career counselors
- Reviewing online job sources such as professional association websites
- Exercising
- Blue-skying/Gazebo building
- Taking courses/getting more education
- Volunteer work
- Having interviews
- Organizing a home office

Even this is an incomplete list. There are 21 items on it, many of which need to be done more than once per week. Let's assume that each task takes two hours. Before you start repeating any of these activities, you already have a 42-hour transition week. That's busy!

People who slow down enough to plan rather than accept the swirl of confusion in their head are generally delighted to discover that their transition calendar is full, not empty. The work of finding work is a job unto itself. There's no time for boredom or depression. The energy expended, far from being fatiguing, actually revitalizes the body, translating all of the positive stress used in rebuilding and channeling it outwards to become the part of the upbeat body language and vibe that makes a positive impression on interviewers and network contacts. And there are further dividends. The people you meet, the education you receive, and the good habits you perfect during the transition period are all transferable to your next position. This period is truly an investment in your future.

THE BUSINESS OF LOOKING FOR WORK

Whether you are currently in, or are facing transition, it will soon come time to dust off the old résumé and see what jobs are on offer, both online and in the paper. Typically, those who think too fast and react too fast are the ones who condemn themselves to extra work and increased hardship during this exercise. For although it is a good idea to ensure your résumé is up to date, it is not the primary tool for getting a good job. *You* are.

It is much more enjoyable and far more productive to do lunch than it is to lick envelopes. I mentioned the value of lunch in terms of networking for the still-employed in the previous chapter, and I mention it again now for the not-currently-employed. Unlike his desk-bound colleagues, a person in transition can actually have two lunches in a day, and a coffee conversation, too. It's not necessary, of course, to eat two lunches' worth of food a day—a salad will do, but an early lunch from 11:30 to 12:30 followed by a later lunch appointment from 12:45 to 1:30, followed by a coffee meeting from 2:00 to 2:30 allows the shrewd networker access to three key superconnectors in a single day.

That's how he'll get the word out. What makes for a shrewd networker?

- He takes the time to choose the right people to have lunch with.
- He makes no bones about his current situation, since there's no stigma to being in transition—it's part of the reality of life.
- He takes the time to schedule these appointments so there is plenty of travel and preparation time between each.
- He takes the time to remember the importance of active listening and then practices it during the conversation.
- He takes the time to remember to talk peer to peer, as equals, remembering that being in transition in no way erases the wisdom, experience, and interest within himself.
- He takes the time to ensure his key message—the type of work or contacts he's looking for—is conveyed effectively to his lunch companion.
- He takes the time to ask his lunch companion what he can do for her. How can he help her business thrive. He keeps the focus on active, outward helping rather than directly asking for help for himself. This is not done with any mercenary intent. He simply asks the same questions he would if he were not in transition: the *cool* questions that a savvy networker would use; the questions that connect with the person he's talking to.
- He takes the time after each meeting to schedule any follow-up activities or calls he has promised to make, including any leads his guest has already given him.

- He takes the time to send a thank-you note to each of his lunch and coffee guests.

Bob Burg, in his book, *Endless Referrals*, reinforces the idea that each person you know knows on average 250 other people.[1] To connect live with one individual is to empower that person to be able to speak on your behalf through the power of personal experience to all of these other people. Having seen you, having interacted with you, having made emotional contact, and having made positive emotional judgments about you, they are in a better position to sell you than a two-page résumé could ever do.

THE HIDDEN JOB MARKET

So, stop waiting for your desired position to be posted or advertised, and go out and get it instead. The best jobs are seldom advertised. In fact, many companies looking for qualified staff approach the search in precisely the opposite way than you would expect.

- First, they'll search from within their own ranks, looking for an internal resource.
- Next, they'll seek out recommendations from internal people (once again proving the value of lifelong networking).
- If that turns up nothing, they'll turn to professionals such as recruiters to find suitable candidates.

Only when these methods fail will they post positions in the Careers section of a newspaper, or on Internet-based career sites. These publications are their last resort. It is up to you, then, to take the time to get to a senior decision maker in that company and tell her about yourself. The job you're looking for may not even exist at present; it may have to be created. But that's not necessarily a problem. If a senior officer sees value in having you aboard, then she will make sure the position is created. The company may not even know that they need you until you tell them. Jeffrey J. Fox, in his wonderful book, *Don't Send a Résumé and Other Contrarian Rules to Help Land a Great Job*, puts it this way:

Each decision influencer and decision-maker has different needs and concerns. Your job is to determine those needs and prove you can satisfy those needs. There is only one reason people hire someone, and that is to solve a problem, calculate the cost to the organization of not solving the problem, and demonstrate that you are the solution.[2]

Time provides the perfect platform upon which to frame that demonstration, and the Internet delivers the material with which to work. You can dig up the dirt on the company, its competitors, the state of the market, upcoming trends—all kinds of things that are publicly available through online sources. This material allows you to identify possible sources of a company's "pain"—the types of things that keep a top executive officer awake at night—which can then be formatted into a well-crafted, one-page pitch letter, or perhaps the agenda of a 15-minute phone call or, better yet, a meeting.

One of the key points that is easy to overlook when moving too fast on this issue is who you need to talk to. It is most likely not the head of HR, unless the solution you're proposing has to do with HR. Most people think they should approach someone in HR, since HR does the hiring. But in actual fact you need to target your approach to the senior officer of the department or area in which you wish to work.

Your goals are to find out who that person is, who her gatekeeper is, and how to get the attention of both of them for five or 10 minutes. This in itself may require a couple of coffee meetings with other people in your network, or perhaps with people in the company itself—people you don't even know but who you could call out of the blue to get pointed in the right direction. Think of the principle of the cheetah described in Chapter 1. Waiting and preparing in order to hunt carefully is a better use of your time than starting immediately and wandering aimlessly.

Case Study: The Dental Firm

Recently I delivered a speech at an annual meeting of a Swiss-based dental technology firm. As I was describing this very point, the concept of hunting down your own job, the senior vice president of the U.S.

division of this company stood up and asked if he could interject. Naturally, I said "sure." He proceeded to ask the assembled group whether they were familiar with the company's vice president of research and development. Yes, everyone knew him. I held my breath. "Well," he said, "that's how he got his VP job. He called me one day out of the blue and pitched me on some ideas and told me about some trends that he foresaw in the market which intrigued me. I wanted to hear more, so I invited him in. That's how he got his job."

This concept represents the art of leveraging the hidden job market. It does not refer to jobs being surreptitiously passed on to cronies in some secret way. This job market is hidden in the same way that a landscape is hidden when you drive past it in a car. You might be traveling faster, sure, but details are lost through speed and height; all you see is blur. When you take the same route by bike, you travel slower, but you see not only trees but the types of trees. You sense subtle changes in climate and terrain, and all things become clearer, including the shortcuts. It's ground-level work that helps the connections get made. It's somewhere between a science and an art: remarkably effective, yet maddeningly unquantifiable. It's slow, yet it's fast.

KEY POINTS TO TAKE AWAY

- *Slow* needs to happen even during transition.
- Building a gazebo refers to the act of undertaking a physical activity in which body and mind are focused on a plan of action that is unrelated to life and its current problems; it's a form of blue-skying.
- Gazebo-building/blue-skying allows for indirect thought, which helps identify alternative methods to describe and market yourself.
- Exercise delivers similar benefits to those of gazebo building and should be considered an essential component of transition as it is in all phases of life.
- An unemployed professional can expect to be out of work one month for every $10,000 she earns or expects to earn annually. This piece of bad news can actually help set a pace and a style of job hunting with better pay-off.
- Lethargy and depression can be warded off simply by taking the time to plan the events required for the work of looking for work. There's too much to do to get depressed.
- The business of looking for work: People in transition who make 100 cold calls or send 100 résumés to 100 addresses may satisfy themselves that they've put in a good day's job hunting, but in fact they've done nothing. They're like people in sales who randomly make cold calls and think the more the better. A more enjoyable and effective approach is to do lunch with people from your network.
- The "hidden job market" refers to the concept of pitching your own job to senior officers rather than waiting for a want ad.

HOW TO *COOL DOWN*

Identify Your Gazebo

- What types of activities do you like to do that encourage creative blue-skying?
- Identify these tasks and schedule them as part of your transition strategy.

Identify Your Unique Identifier

- What term or sentence could you use to describe your work in a memorable way?
- Remember, other people who are not in your line of work will find great interest in the things you consider normal or boring.
- Does your line of work appeal to certain demographics, e.g., sports enthusiasts, frequent travelers, parents? What can you do to upsell your interest factor during conversation?
- Practice your unique identifiers until you can deliver them with confidence and credibility.

Strategize Your Optimum Meeting Times

- When do you think the best time to meet with people for formal interviews would be? 10:30 a.m.? 9:00 a.m.? 4:00 p.m.?
- Who could you ask to find out?

Exercise

- When is your preferred time to exercise? Morning? Afternoon? Schedule this into your daily schedule for at least four days out of five.

Schedule

- What system will you use to time manage your transition period? Microsoft Outlook? A DayTimer? Your PDA?
- Keep in mind the work of finding work is a job unto itself. It requires planning and *slow* thought just as any other job would.

Hunt Down Your Next Job

- Where would you like to work next?
- What do you value?
- What does your next job look like?
- What hours and conditions would suit you best?
- What do you wish to achieve in your next job?
- What companies interest you?
- What industries interest you?
- What departments interest you?
- Use the answers from these questions to target your next possible employer.
- Research the company or companies you wish to work for.
- Research the executives and officers.
- Set to work, like a detective, to find out how you can get 15 minutes with these people.
- Remember, company executives are looking for "bright sparks" who can either make the company money or save the company money. Which can you do?
- How can you sell your ideas to them?

1   Burg, Bob, *Endless Referrals*, Third Edition, McGraw-Hill, 2005
2   Fox, Jeffrey, *Don't Send a Résumé: And Other Contrarian Rules to Help Land a Great Job.* Hyperion Books, 2001, p. 87

WE ALL WORK SO HARD

FOR THE GOOD OF OUR CHILDREN,

WHO WANT US TO PLAY.

CHAPTER 11
THE FAMILY

If there was ever a need for *slow* in the business day, it most definitely has to be where family is concerned. No matter what form your family takes: one parent, two parents, young kids, old kids, step-kids, sandwich families with elders in the house, even couples or singles with no kids at all, the ambient momentum of speed at work invariably filters through into home life.

TRYING TO BE BOTH A PROFESSIONAL AND A PARENT

It's tough enough getting through all of the challenges described in the previous chapters without having to deal with the emotional and logistical challenges of being part of a family. But children are shrewd observers. They need to be taught about the value of *slow* in action as well as concept. They need to be shown that, as a complement to their busy lives, they must include time for reflection, communication, and thought. Kids learn a heck of a lot through observation. Just as they learned to walk and talk by watching their parents or older sibling(s), so will they learn the value of work, rest, and discipline. If they see Mom returning emails at all hours of the night, or carrying her wireless PDA to bed, they, too will learn the repressive ways of the harness. This threatens to build another generation of hard-working people for whom creativity is pushed aside in order to fit a tight schedule into the day.

As we've seen throughout this book, jobs are changing. Employability, career determination, career preservation, flexibility, and "hunting ability" will be based on talents more profound than on how many emails a person can return. Plumbers and accountants, for example, will always be needed, but if a young future plumber or accountant is not shown how important it is to allow adequate time for doing things other than the tasks at hand—marketing and maintaining her business, for example, along with seeking out a balanced life—her business will not survive.

So this is what this chapter is about: How to *cool down* enough to ensure that families of any size and configuration can avoid getting lost upon the featureless sea of busy-ness.

DINNER: A TIME TO COOL DOWN

One possible *cool* approach to avoiding the challenge of remaining adrift in this sea is to use dinner as a safe harbor. Dinnertime often suffers when there are so many other activities and priorities that regularly interfere. But as I have demonstrated elsewhere in this book, the payoff to *cooling down* is not only in the immediate: What you eat is not the most important part of dinner; it's what you do with the time. You could even order in, or dine out, if budget allows.

Blue Flag Day

For a regular dinner to stand a chance against the pressures of busy workdays and busy evenings, you need to employ tangible tools. One interesting technique is what I call "Blue Flag Day." This is based on a simple promise that you make to your family. "For two evenings during the Monday-to-Friday week, our family (whatever size or configuration) will dine together." This could be put forth as a suitable compromise, one that recognizes the numerous demands foisted upon individual family members during the after-work and after-school periods: extracurricular sports, for example, as well as homework and socializing. These extracurricular activities are important in themselves, of course, but it's just too easy for people of all ages to fall prey to the temptation to quickly gulp down food and return to other diversions. At least with just two dinners a week reserved, the opportunity exists to balance scheduled events such as games, meetings, and practices with equally important family dinners together.

The best way for a family to implement and maintain this two-dinner workweek is to use the power of symbolism. Call it a blue flag day. Set it up on a calendar on the fridge and enter it into all the DayTimers, PDAs, and cellphone calendars of each family member: Identify the dates when these suppers are to happen and then highlight the two one-hour blocks in blue as a "must attend." On the day of the dinner you can place blue placemats or napkins on the morning breakfast table to serve as an additional reminder of the upcoming evening get-together. During the blue flag dinners themselves, turn off the TV and put away all other personal devices such as music players and PDAs. Don't answer the phone unless call-display identifies the caller as a key person, for example, an extended family member who might be calling for help.

Now the use of this blue symbolism might seem extreme to some, and there are many families who might not need to go to these lengths in order to have a quiet, regular dinner. But there are many others for whom time and busy-ness have stripped away opportunities for regular togetherness and have inserted a habit of continuous busy-ness instead. For them, the use of imagery, in this case the color blue (it could be any other color or image), can be a powerful technique that will help reconstruct the concept of dinner as a tangible thing. Imagery helps to influence us through tangible means. This can apply equally well to single people who wish to maintain meaningful relationships with friends and partners or to large, extended families and everything in between. Relationships are based upon and reinforced by time together as well as time apart. Unfortunately, spending time in this way often gets pushed aside and is too often viewed as negligible personal time, just like lunch and exercise time.

As I said before, it's not the food that counts, it's the time. Blue flag dinners allow for essential things to happen:

- Talking about good things. Each family member is able to speak up about positive events or achievements of the day. They are able to be heard, and they are able to hear themselves talking about their ideas and issues. This is another example of dual mentorship: being heard, while hearing yourself speak.
- Talking about bad things. The dinner allows time and a safe venue for the outlet of pent-up frustrations.
- Learning about each other's days and issues.
- Learning about upcoming events and deadlines and ensuring all calendars are up to date.

Beyond these initial achievements, blue flag dinners offer other essential benefits that parents might find valuable:

- Observing subtleties. Family dinners, like all face-to-face interactions, make it easier to pick up on subtle facial gestures, eye movements, and other cues that might hint at deeper issues needing to be resolved.
- Mannerisms and social etiquette. Mastering social techniques such as how to correctly use a knife and fork, how to serve food and drink, or how to hold a conversation while eating are skills that are not taught in a cafeteria or food-court but may make or break a future work opportunity. There's no better place to learn them than in the supportive environment of a family dinner.
- The reinforcement of stability through regularity. As many family psychologists will attest, the ritual of regular family dinners has the potential to penetrate even the most cynical or confused teenage hide, to deliver a message of consistency and reliability about themselves and about their family. Though teenagers often fall prey to the desire to rebel, the knowledge that there is regularity in their world, even as they try to rebel against it, is a comfort they might not want to admit to but will be aware of all the same.

- Building attention spans and focus through routine. The concept of "attention deficit," whether diagnosed as a disorder or not, is a growing phenomenon in North American kids. For some people there may indeed be clinical sources to this disorder, but for many others problems related to keeping focused might have something to do with the variability and pace of life itself. Part of the problem may be blamed on TV and video games, but what about the lack of evening routines? In infant years regular routines of feeding, bathing, and storytelling helped develop regular sleeping patterns and helped foster intellectual growth. However, as kids grow from infants into youngsters, regularity is cast aside to fit in more activities. I have already discussed in Chapter 1, the value of sleep, and in particular the chemistry involved in the winding-down hours prior to sleep. Might not the regularity and slowness of at least two dinners per week help to counter the same type of chemical chaos found in over-stimulated children?

THE LEGITIMACY OF DOING NOTHING FOR A WHILE

Another benefit that the blue flag dinner offers to all participants, regardless of age, is that of legitimizing the act of "doing nothing" for a short while. This reinforces the value and power of silence, or at least, stillness. You *are* doing something, of course, you're eating and talking and listening. But for this hour, you are not playing soccer, working on the computer, or talking on the phone. You are just being—together.

This, I believe, goes a long way towards teaching kids and adults alike that it's all right to stop for a while, that event-to-event living comes at a great cost, and that pausing occasionally yields its own dividends. While there's good intention in sending your kids to one extracurricular activity after another, there is also the danger of conditioning them by way of this experience that to race from event-to-event is the sole approach to working life. For some parents at least, the desire to see kids involved and active, combined with their own momentum and event-to-event thinking might have swung the pendulum a little too far to one side—to the point at which there is so much going on that time for decompression is completely lost.

Some parents, of course, might see nothing wrong with this, since activity keeps kids healthy and active. Similarly, adults without kids, who find themselves too busy for blue-flag dinners with partners and friends, might satisfy themselves that a busy life equals a fulfilled life. But once again, this reveals an addiction to immediacies that robs all of us of deeper, more profound understanding. Take, for example, the concept of accountability.

HOW PAUSE LEADS TO ACCOUNTABILITY

Event-to-event blindness, as I have demonstrated, leads to a kind of intellectual isolation. When people are given no time to pause, reflect, and process the stresses of the day, their sense of isolation deepens. For example, when we observe a person exhibiting road rage or merely driving aggressively, we observe that person demonstrate anger over having his route interrupted, his dignity supposedly mocked. An eruption occurs within the isolation of his event-to-event existence. Isolation, as the Dalai Lama points out in *The Art of Happiness*, magnifies suffering,[1] and a magnification of suffering quickly leads to overreaction. But it is quicker and easier, it seems, to accept this isolation as a fact of life and just keep moving. This is what Boxer the horse did in *Animal Farm*, described in our very first chapter.

Acceptance of bad habits leads to their legitimization. Observe, for example, how road rage has now been redefined clinically, as a condition called Intermittent Explosive Disorder (IED). Does everyone who claims to have IED actually have it, or are they just having a bad day or a bad week or a bad drive home? This legitimization of IED has been met with skepticism from some mental health professionals and social psychologists alike. The problem, they say, is that accepting road rage as a clinical condition tends to take the accountability for such behavior away from the individual and place it somewhere in the misty realms of society at large.

But why am I discussing road rage here, in a section about dining together as a family? Because the clinical legitimization of IED symbolizes a growing trend in the erosion of personal accountability, a trend that can be countered through simple, *slow* rituals such as pausing for dinner.

Let's see if there are other connections that can be made to support this idea:

- Email. We've talked a lot about email in this book. One of the major problems with email is that people send letters and attachments before they're truly thought-out and ready, so as to get that particular task off their desk in order to make room for the next one. The decision as to whether the letter is ready, appropriate, and serves the purpose is moot. It's now out there in the system—the loop. It's somebody else's problem. The accountability for the appropriateness of that letter has been eliminated through the *ambient momentum* of the workplace. But will this letter elicit a proper, timely response? Will it do its job effectively?

- Meetings. A person needs to schedule a meeting with a number of her colleagues. Knowing that no-one will be happy being forced into a meeting, she books the meeting online, allowing the software itself to inform the participants about the meeting. The potential difficulty of confronting these people has now been avoided. Accountability for ensuring a level of buy-in and participation from those around the table has been avoided. But will such techniques foster true collaboration and trust in the future?

- The accountant described in Chapter 3 puts off delivering bad news to his client by occupying himself with other tasks. Anything to avoid the confrontation with his client that he knows will be difficult. Accountability for creative human problem solving has been ducked. But will it lead to further business or referrals?

High-speed pressure tends to squeeze out of people the willingness and ability to account for their own actions and to be responsible for both the good and the bad in life. Is it any surprise, then, that accountability for road rage has now conveniently been shifted away from the individual himself? Or that coffee shops and fast food restaurants can be successfully sued for serving hot beverages? The loss of personal accountability threatens to rob society of innovators, leaders, and motivated individuals, and to rob individuals themselves of the gifts of self-determination and of questioning the world around them. We can prevent a great deal of this evasion of responsibility simply by ensuring time is spent with people we care about. This solution applies equally well to large families as it does to singles, and everyone in between. Make sure to make time to talk with people who can hear you, while you simultaneously hear yourself. Let the pressures of life find a slower, safer escape route.

NO TIME TO BE THE "BAD GUY"

Consider also the dilemma many overworked parents face in having to be the "bad guy" when discipline is required. When you come home from work late and there's only half an hour between the time you pull into the driveway and the time the kids go to bed, who wants to spend that time being stern? Well-intentioned parents know that discipline and guidance is necessary, of course, but that doesn't make it any easier. When there's little time to transition from the pressures of the workplace and those of home, the quality of the parent-child relationship suffers.

Discipline, like accountability, is like medicine inside a bitter pill— hard to take but essential to well-being. Children who do not grow up with the discipline of regular homework, supper, and bedtime hours, and then miss out on the rules and corrections that parents are duty-bound to give, will emerge unwittingly with a gaping hole where personal accountability should be. This is already evident in the spate of lawsuits recently launched against teachers and schools who fail a student or who give a B when an A was desired. Is a low mark the fault of the student or the school? A loss of personal accountability guarantees that blame will be placed in someone else's hands.

Though the above examples focus largely on the relationship between kids and their parents, the same principles apply to other types of relationships, too. Observe the following case study:

Case Study: The Hit-and-Run Cyclist

In the summer of 2006, an elderly man exited from a health club where he had been enjoying his daily seniors' exercise workout. As he did so, a cyclist who was traveling on the sidewalk, crashed into him. The senior was knocked to the ground and suffered injuries to his head and face. Instead of apologizing or offering to help, the cyclist berated the old man, accusing him of getting in his way, and criticizing him for walking so slowly. The cyclist then took off, and it was left to a couple of good Samaritans to help the man to a hospital, where he was admitted for observation. This is certainly not an isolated case, but it highlights the type of thing that easily happens when immediate reactionism rules.

NO TIME TO BE A KID

Another reason for the need to *cool down* within the family portion of the 24-hour day has to do simply with overload. Children of all ages have schedules and distractions as much as any adult.

Nw i ly me dn2slp

Kids have already learned the addictive ways of the high-speed life and they don't want to (or can't) give it up. Sixty percent of children over eight years old in the UK carry cell phones, as do 90 percent of kids over age 12. There's even a special ringtone used by kids who desire unfettered access, set at a frequency that adults over the age of 20 can't hear.[2] Such devices are being used by kids all day—during class, and especially after bed-time, when active chatting and text messaging take the place of sleep.

A story in the *Globe and Mail* newspaper described the problem like this:

> "Even before they get off the bus, they're already tired, and in class ... they're kind of dragging their heels and not as alert," said Vancouver teacher Sharon Wyatt. ...Yet parents themselves may be partly responsible for their children being constantly sleepy. ... Many who work late will deliberately keep their youngsters up so they can spend time together.
>
> Studies show [that sleep-deprived children] are more likely to suffer higher rates of learning difficulties, behavioral

problems, obesity, illness, accidents ... lower levels of concentration, attention spans and creativity, a loss of short-term memory and an increase in hyperactivity.

Some sleep-deprived youngsters are even misdiagnosed with attention-deficit hyperactivity disorder and could be unnecessarily medicated, said Dr. Val Kirk, medical director of the Pediatric Sleep Service at Alberta Children's Hospital in Calgary. "There's a lot of overlap ... between some of the symptoms." [3]

It's hard to keep up with all of this, but that's why *slowing down* is so important. Think what a mom or dad who adopts some of the principles of *slow* could do for the kids at home:

- Developing the skills to manage at-work workload *becomes* the ability to help a child plan for and complete homework, assignments, and study for exams.
- Establishing pace and balance to ensure the right work gets done the right way *becomes* the ability to teach a child the art of prioritization and clear thinking.
- Recognizing and discussing the value of having a mentor *becomes* an opportunity for the child to understand that she, too, can open up and talk with her parents about problems or difficulties.
- Eating a good morning breakfast *becomes* proof of its importance and legitimacy.
- Preparing and packing a good lunch into Mom and Dad's briefcase *becomes* a demonstration that eating and preparing meals is not a tedious chore but a legitimate and important component of the day.
- Eliminating the temptation to bring work home or to spend home time reading emails and text messages *becomes* a demonstration that work and life need balance and that it is in everyone's grasp.
- Eliminating the temptation to bring work home or to spend home time reading emails and text messages *also becomes* an opportunity to help a child's study efforts by asking him what he

now *knows* about what he's just read. Learning is best achieved not by simply reading something but by talking about it after.

- Eliminating the temptation to bring work home or to spend home time reading emails and text messages *also becomes* an opportunity to observe a child's Internet usage, especially when chat rooms are involved.

Tips for Transitioning between Work and Home

- Use the commute or the drive as decompression time. Leave the cell phone in the briefcase and listen to music, or just blue-sky.
- Develop a habit of closure at the office. Use the last few minutes at work to close down your email and to change your daily voice mail greeting to tomorrow's date. This helps define the end of a day.
- If tensions from work follow you home, use a "trouble tree." Based on a traditional poem, a trouble tree is a tree, a bush, or any other object located just outside the front door upon which people "hang" their work troubles before entering the house. Pause a moment to picture this before you walk through the door. Not only does this help avoid bringing stresses upon the family, but, as the parable goes, many of the troubles tend to get blown off the tree overnight.

THE POWER OF THE PAUSE

In the 1960s an experiment was done to learn just how long a person can go without sleep. A student volunteer, Randy Gardner, was kept awake and active by a rotation of experimenters, who kept him busy doing quizzes and physical coordination tests. He was able to stay involved for nine days before succumbing to total fatigue. Nine days. The interesting thing about this, however, was that once he was allowed to sleep, he slept for just 14 hours and then woke up fully refreshed. His brain and body, just like ours, was able to recover and refresh in a time period far less than the equivalent of nine nights' worth of sleep.

This story illustrates very vividly the value of downtime in all of our lives. An evening with friends or family will do more for your intellect, and therefore your career, than will another all-nighter over the computer. A lunch away from your desk and away from your work will do more for your daylight productivity than will lunch over the keyboard. Calling an official end to the day sets in place the terrific recuperative faculties that all of us contain, physically, inside of us.

This book is obviously about the value of slowing down, primarily in the workplace. This last chapter extends briefly into home life simply to demonstrate how valuable *cooling down* can be for everyone—busy working people as well as their families and friends. Not everyone has school-age kids, of course, but everyone has people with whom they and enjoy mutual support. Are you making enough time in your day, or week, or year to ensure that these people get the best from you—and that you get the best from them? Are the tasks and pressures that you currently face sufficiently important to justify placing these people second or third? Or do these all-consuming tasks just *seem* to be so? Do you have the ability to negotiate alternate dates, deadlines, and deliveries? Can you relate to your manager or customers in such a way as to give yourself permission to go home on a timely basis?

This book is intended to give advice and suggestions, based on observations and case studies. It's hard to be told what to do by someone you don't know, especially when things get personal, when family is involved. But in preparing this book, my mind often reverts to the story of the lawyer described in Chapter 9, who regretted his successful life due to its cost.

I am reminded also of a client of mine with whom I worked some years ago who had spent most of his early professional life, from age 25 to 40, circling the globe on behalf of his employer. Visiting district offices on every continent, and living out of a suitcase, he built a successful career that he then promptly walked away from.

I asked him why he did it. He told me it was the day he stayed home for a weekend to spend some time with his new infant daughter who was then six months old. As much as he tried, his daughter did not want to stay on his lap. She screamed to get off because she didn't know who he was. He could not feed her, pick her up, or even look into her eyes. She was too afraid—of her own father. Not shy, afraid.

That was the day he discovered that the cost of his career had become too great. He had to make a change, and that's just what he did. But he did not have to quit his job, nor take a sabbatical or even a cut in pay. All he had to do—all he did do, was to sit down with his manager and discuss where things had got to. He simply talked with his manager, who himself had been too busy to truly notice the recent increase in travel, and together they worked on a renewed, refined plan of operations, in which the needs of the company were met, yet which allowed for a more balanced, healthy lifestyle for my colleague.

KEY POINTS TO TAKE AWAY

- Mealtime is a prime opportunity for decompression and for active listening with your family. It is often sacrificed due to the demands of high-speed, extra-curricular activities.
- Techniques such as "blue flag" day are intended to reinforce positive habits through symbolism and regularity.
- There is great legitimacy in "doing nothing" for a while.
- One of the dangers of high-speed living and of its social acceptance is the elimination of accountability.
- Busy parents also hesitate at playing the "bad guy" when their time with their kids is already limited.
- Kids learn by observing. If they see Mom or Dad returning emails at all hours of the night, they will adopt the same lifestyle.
- Kids have already adopted the high-speed lifestyle through late-night access to text messaging.
- The human body has a tremendous capacity to recuperate and regenerate in a short time. Use the power of the pause to add to, not take away from, your potential.

HOW TO *COOL DOWN*

- Schedule your "together times" as far in advance as possible. Use your calendars to highlight these dates and times. Use colors or other symbolism to make them as real as possible.
- Choose symbolism that works for you.
- Use the same techniques at work. Use your office calendar to highlight times that you will be unavailable, e.g., 4:30 p.m. onwards on a blue flag day.
- Use your ability to influence other people to ensure they know about your comparatively early departure on select days.
- Practice the art of decompressing. Can you put your cell phone aside during your drive home? Choose a selection of music or spoken-word novels instead.
- Practice the art of leaving work troubles outside. Identify an object that exists outside your residence upon which you can metaphorically "hang" your troubles.
- Schedule special dates such as birthdays and anniversaries into your calendar, but be sure also to include lead time, such as a reminder seven days ahead which will give you time to buy and mail cards or gifts or to make restaurant reservations.
- Make sure to schedule these dates as recurring items, so you don't forget next year.
- Call one person from your circle of friends each week just to say hello.
- Remember the parable of the sleep-deprivation student—a little pause or refreshment is all you need.

---

1 The Dalai Lama, *The Art of Happiness: A Handbook for Living*. Riverhead, 1998.
2 "Children's bedtimes getting later—and later." *The Globe and Mail*, April 8, 2006.
3 Ibid.

CONCLUSION

When I first heard about and then researched the *Slow* movement, the various aspects of my persona—the engineer, the industrial psychologist, the teacher, the business owner, the parent—all demanded to know whether the concepts as described by the *Slow* movement's aficionados could be accepted in any form by the speed-loving, debt-plagued citizens of the Western world.

I have attempted to answer yes—we must adopt the principles of *slow* if we are to remain competitive, employable, and healthy, both collectively and, more importantly, as individuals. I have met many people who have already successfully adopted and adapted the principles of *slow* into their lives. They have shown me how they've been able to communicate better with their teams, close more sales, delegate, influence, become more creative, sleep better, eat better, maintain a healthy weight, connect with their families, expand their circle of friends and business acquaintances, build their career safety net, enjoy a balanced life, and much, much more, simply by introducing *cool down* concepts in careful increments; by planning carefully, communicating clearly, and encouraging a greater amount of human-to-human intellectual and emotional contact.

Whenever I question my legitimacy as a writer and a time management expert as to whether I have the right to say the things I say in this book, I think of my colleague, the world traveller, whose daughter didn't know him. I think of the lawyer who had had no life, and I think of all the other people I have met who would admit, if pressed, that perhaps, yes, they've let the harness stay on longer than it ought.

I think also of all the others I know, or know of, who have found success, in whatever manner they define that term, by taking the time to do it right.

If you are considering joining this latter group, by embracing some of the principles and practices mentioned in this book, be sure to write your ideas down, to get them out of your head (so as not to forget them *and* to make room for more). Then talk about them. Talk to a mentor. Talk to your manager. You can even write to me, if you'd like (just go to www.bristall.com and use the *Contact Us* link).

Then practice until you get it right. *Cooling down* is possible. It is healthier, and it will get you where you want to go, faster, and in better condition. Life's just too short to live at high speed.

INDEX

ABOUT THE AUTHOR

© As It Happens Photography

Steve Prentice is president of Bristall Morgan Inc., a professional education firm with offices in Toronto and New York City, which specializes in reinstating productivity and profitability where distraction and overload currently reign. His first book is entitled *Cool Time: A Hands-on Plan for Managing Work and Balancing Time* and is published by John Wiley and Sons (2005). He is a frequent media guest and is regularly called on for TV and radio interviews to discuss issues dealing with stress, overload, and workplace technology.